EAT WHERE YOU LIVE

EAT WHERE YOU LIVE

How to find and

enjoy local and

sustainable food no

matter where you live

LOU BENDRICK

SKIPSTONE

Published by Skipstone, an imprint of The Mountaineers Books
Printed in the United States of America

First printing 2008
10 09 08 07   5 4 3 2 1

Copy Editor: Alice Copp Smith
Design: Mayumi Thompson
Cover photograph: © Veer

Hardiness Zones Map on page 62 © 2006 by The National Arbor Day Foundation

Juneberry Muffins recipe on pages 90–91 reprinted with permission from *Wild Plants I Have Known ... and Eaten* by Russ Cohen

Food Storage Chart on pages 108–116 excerpted from "Enjoy Fresh, Local Food All Year" by Barbara Pleasant, *Mother Earth News* magazine, August 2007. Read the full story at www.motherearthnews.com or call (800)234-3368 to subscribe. © 2008 Ogden Publications, Inc.

Library of Congress Cataloging-in-Publication Data
Bendrick, Lou.
  Eat where you live : how to find and enjoy local and sustainable food no matter where you live / by Lou Bendrick. — 1st ed.
      p. cm.
  Includes bibliographical references and index.
  1. Sustainable agriculture. 2. Food supply. 3. Natural foods. I. Title.
  S494.5.S86B46 2008
  641.3'1—dc22

                          2008027074

ISBN 978-1-59485-074-5

Skipstone
1001 SW Klickitat Way
Suite 201
Seattle, Washington 98134
206.223.6303
www.skipstonepress.org
www.mountaineersbooks.org

LIVE LIFE. MAKE RIPPLES.

For Hal, Annie, Coulter, and Simon

CONTENTS

ACKNOWLEDGMENTS

This book would not have been possible without Dana Youlin, my editor at Skipstone, who must possess fairy magic because she convinced me to take on this book while I was pregnant. Her support, kindness, preternatural calm and insight through-out the process were invaluable—I couldn't ask any more of an editor. Indeed, in the era of giant publishers, I am lucky to have landed at Skipstone, where everyone I encountered—the sensitive and intellectually rigorous Alice Smith, the organized and kindly Margaret Sullivan, and the enthusiastic Shanna Knowlton—made my book better. Of course, the book would not have been possible without the inspiration and suste-nance that comes from the farmers who feed my family and me. These hardworking, lovely people include Sean Stanton at North Plain and Blue Hill Farms, whose eggs changed my life and who always, and with good cheer and patience, answered my questions (in the freezing rain . . . on a cell phone . . . while feeding hogs). Also thanks to Dominic Palumbo at the beautiful Moon in the Pond Farm, who makes me laugh and whose hot dogs are a revelation. Also Elizabeth Keen and Al Thorp at Indian Line Farm, my CSA, who are patient, friendly, and kind and whose immaculate and picturesque farm is one of the best parts of living in the Berkshires. Thanks, too, to all of the people I pestered and peppered with questions and who granted me their precious time: Tod Murphy, Russ Cohen, Hank Lentfer, Clare Butterfield, Marc David, Barbara Zheutlin, Matt Rubiner, Tara Miner. Yikes, people! You're all super! This working mom would also be remiss in not thanking Heidi Burger, the world's best babysitter. To Karl Warkomski, my friend since kindergarten: Thanks for being my personal eco-guru and garden expert. Of course, the biggest debt of gratitude is to you, Hal, my husband and best friend, not to mention personal editorial director, mentor, muse, and one hell of a good cook. Kiss-kiss! Kisses to you, too, Annie, my smart, sweet, farm-going daughter, who sometimes sat next to me, patiently drawing while I typed. Thanks also, baby Coulter, for being a consistent napper during this whole process. Other family thanks go to Marty Carlock—my cheerleader and a wonderful MIL. Thanks, too, to anyone I left out—this is by necessity only a partial list of all the wonderful people who contributed. Last, but certainly not least, thanks, Simon, my trusty canine assistant: You are a good boy, oh, yes you are. I'm going to get off this silly computer and take you for a walk now.

INTRODUCTION

I KNOW WHAT'S ON YOUR MIND AND HAVE AN EGGSTATIC RESPONSE

Just a wild guess here: If you're reading this book, you are already convinced that sustainable and local food can be a fantastic part of your life (either that or your sister-in-law gave you the book and you're flipping through it just to be polite). Another guess: Your enthusiasm and curiosity are a little tempered by nagging questions such as *Even if I can get my hands on sustainable and local food, how much work is this going to be? Am I going to go broke eating this way? Why bother when I can just get everything I need in one fell swoop at the local Safeway?*

Wow. You are so normal.

You are going to have to trust me—if I can do this, so can you. I'm an all-American, frantically busy, caffeine-dependent, cell-phone-toting, iPod-loving mother of two. I'm not a yuppie, hippie, green-thumber, or food professional (just ask my husband). Nor do I eat all local foods all the time—not even close. My hat is off is to those resourceful people who do so, but for most of us, it's not an option. But including local foods in our everyday diets should be an easy option for all of us.

Now then: Forgive me for the Socratic method here, but I'll answer your nagging (and very good) questions by asking you a question:

When was the last time you ate cookie batter?

I'm guessing that it has been a long time—most likely since your childhood—since you've tasted cookie dough outside of an ice cream cone. That's because eating raw or undercooked eggs these days is a dangerous practice—just read the small print on restaurant menus. I went several years without eating a single egg because, in 2001, I got salmonellosis, an infection caused by a bacterium called *Salmonella* that can come from raw or undercooked eggs. (Mine came from an undercooked scrambled egg.) If you've never had salmonella poisoning, let me say this about that: It might not kill you, but you'll wish it would. After I recovered, I not only stopped eating eggs but also treated every egg that came through my door like a biohazard. My poor husband couldn't make an omelet without me lurking about with a Clorox wipe, which does not set exactly the right tone for a leisurely brunch.

My attitude toward eggs changed several years later when I discovered sustainable and local eggs—henceforth known as "my eggs." They are sustainable because they do not degrade, deplete, or pollute the land or its inhabitants, but instead come from kindly raised, fluffy hens who are never fed hormones or antibiotics. They're local because they come from a farm three miles from my doorstep. But I'm not going out of my way to get these eggs in order to adhere to a politically correct definition. I go out of my way because I made the happy discovery that going to a farm beats pushing a squeaky-wheeled cart through the two-mile breakfast cereal aisle. On my "egg runs," my daughter and I have patted the heads of fuzzy chicks, watched newborn piglets squeal and run, visited with horses and goats, and watched ducks make the most of mud puddles. Bottom line: **My eggs are fun.**

But it doesn't stop there. My eggs—*free-range, pastured eggs*—are higher in brain-boosting omega-3 fatty acids, Vitamins A and E, folic acid, and beta carotene, and lower in cholesterol to boot—than commercially raised eggs. Because my eggs are truly fresh and come from healthy chickens (which I have seen with my own two eyes) and not from the intensive overcrowded conditions in factory farms, I am not worried about getting sick from them. Am I eating raw eggs with abandon? Of course not. But I'm also not putting on a hazmat suit to scramble them. My point: **My eggs are healthy.**

True, I could just buy healthy eggs with an organic label. Don't get me wrong: Organic is a very good thing, and I'm not here to bash it. An organic label means that our government has deemed the food is free from certain harmful pesticides, hormones, and drugs. In the case of eggs, "organic" means that they come from chickens whose food contains minimal amounts of herbicides, fungicides, pesticides, and commercial fertilizers. But there's a reason why "local is the new organic." Keeping my egg farmer in business means that he'll be less likely to sell his farm, as tempting as that may be, to make room for condos or another strip mall. It also means that the money I spend on eggs goes directly to a farmer in my community and not to some giant corporation in a town I've never heard of. My farmer is now also my friend, and who couldn't use another friend in this crazy mixed-up world? Astonishing but true: **My eggs build community.**

Another consideration: My eggs haven't been trucked long distances to get to my plate. Eating locally eliminates other negative effects of long-haul trucking: air pollution, the burning of fossil fuels, and that obnoxious sound trucks make with something called a *jake brake*. In their own small way: **My eggs are a bit gentler on the planet.**

All this is well and good, but you might be wondering if I am taking out a second mortgage to shop for groceries. It's true, I spend a whopping $4 on a dozen eggs, which makes most people faint (even after I point out that they routinely spend more than two dollars on a single latte). Frugal type, stay thy hand: You'd never settle for a substandard car seat for your child, so why would you feed her a substandard egg? I beg you to remember that cheap food is a stinker of a lie because of its "hidden costs": the cost to your health (from hormones, pesticides, trans fats, and so on) and the cost to the planet (from pesticides, pollution, etc.). By eating a bit more locally and spending less time in the typical gargantuan grocery store, I spend less money on packaged foods and impulse items (such as those well-placed chocolate bars at the checkout) and gravitate toward simpler, seasonal recipes. It's shocking but true: **My eggs save me money.**

But let's face it: Time is money. Cooking real meals from real food takes a little time, but not tons of time. Take chocolate chip cookies, for example: They don't take all day. At the most, they take an hour (less if you make your kitchen slaves, I mean children, help with the dishes). Can packaged cookies even compare to the smell, let alone the taste, of a batch of hot cookies on a cold afternoon? I think you know where I'm going here: **My eggs are worth a little extra time.**

Last, and perhaps most important: If sustainable and local foods didn't taste better than conventionally grown, fast, cheap, processed foods, none of the above would matter. My eggs, with their glossy orange yolks, produce sublime desserts and inspire leisurely brunches. They are *eggy* eggs. One taste of them and you know you've been robbed by all those years of eating those ersatz white oval things. To sum: **My eggs taste great.**

But don't take my word for it. Let me help you find and enjoy some incredible eggs, and other sustainable food, for yourself. Because cookie batter shouldn't be a thing to fear.

Chapter One

DOWN ON THE FARM: WHERE TO FIND SUSTAINABLE FOOD

or many years, finding sustainable and local foods was mostly serendipity as I stumbled upon farmers markets or drove past a farm stand here and there. Then, in 2003, I moved to western Massachusetts and discovered that it was an incredible "foodshed." (This term means the area that provides my food. You'll find a whole lot more Scrabble terms like it in the Glossary.) Here I discovered Berkshire Grown, a local food advocacy organization that produces a map to farms, farmers markets, and other food producers. Now, despite the fact that I am incapable of folding maps correctly, finding local food couldn't be easier. Depending on where you live, things might not be so cinchy. This is why I've created some tips on finding local food—and making sure it's sustainable, too.

FARMS, U-PICKS, AND FARM STANDS

Let's go straight to the source of fresh food! Yes, my friends, I'm talking about going to that archetypal place of chickens and silos: the farm itself. Going to the farm not only allows you to see firsthand whether your food is sustainably produced, but it's also a welcome break from listening to the Muzak version of Bob Dylan songs at your grocery store. But where can you find a farm that might welcome your city-slicking presence? Try the following tactics.

Surf the Internet. Get thee to thy favorite search engine and plug in keywords such as "local food" and your state. Chances are that your state has its own agency and website to promote in-state agricultural products. You can also get more specific and plug in words such as "turnips" and your county or town to narrow the search. Some regions have their own local food advocacy groups. In addition to your own sleuthing, don't miss some of the biggest online local food databases:

- For meat and dairy, be sure to try The Sustainable Table's website, www.sustainabletable.org. The Sustainable Table, which provides a wealth of information about why and how to buy sustainable meat and dairy products, will also show you where to buy them through its "Eat Well Guide," which is easily searchable by zip code: www.eatwellguide.org.
- Don't miss the easy-to-use LocalHarvest's nationwide database to find organic food and products from farms, farmers markets, restaurants, stores, and co-ops close to you. If you can't find organic food near you, shop from the catalog: www.localharvest.org.
- The Rodale Institute's New Farm website, which is aimed at sustainable food producers, has a feature for consumers. The "Farm Locator" allows you to search for farms or markets in your area. Plus, you can narrow your search by category, such as "farm stand": www.newfarm.org/farmlocator/index.php.
- Ask Bob. Are you really stumped when it comes to connecting to a local food network? Go to Foodroutes .org (www.foodroutes.org) and ask "Food Lovin' Bob," their online expert, to help you. Foodroutes, which collaborated on the LocalHarvest database, can also help you understand where your food comes from and why it's important to buy fresh and local. Its grassroots "Buy Fresh Buy Local" chapters throughout the United States promote sustainable agriculture.

Roadside Butterfat on a Cone

Back in the day (I promise never to use that phrase again), summertime wasn't marked by pedicures (not that pretty toes are a bad thing) but by watermelon, sweet corn, and melting ice cream you had to lick off of your arm. For many people, summer ice cream, rich in butterfat, was purchased at roadside ice cream stands (in my neck of the woods, sometimes called "creamie" or "custard" stands) that were often affiliated with a local dairy. If you're lucky and a bit industrious, you can still find one. The Internet is a good source of info for locating such stands, but the best source, of course, is an actual local who knows when the stand opens and what special flavor to try (maple is popular in New England).

Don't forget to ask whether or not the milk has hormones or antibiotics in it. My protective-momma rule of thumb: If the milk isn't organic, I ask whether or not it contains "growth hormones." What I'm really looking for is whether or not the milk contains rBGH (recombinant bovine growth hormone), a genetically engineered substance given to cows to increase milk production. Canada and the European Union have banned rBGH due to safety concerns. Don't be embarrassed to ask these questions about your double dip of butter pecan. Even if you get a blank look from the person scooping your ice cream, remember that your question is a form of demand—and demand drives the market. (Ah, feel the power!)

Surf the phone book. If a computer is not an option, let your fingers do the walking. Try the phone book's Yellow Pages, using keywords such as "farm" or "food coop," or contact your local chamber of commerce. Also, thumb over to the local government listings to find a Cooperative Extension Service. Cooperative extensions not only are responsible for 4-H clubs but are staffed by experts from land-grant universities who provide information to agricultural communities. Whether you live in an agricultural community or not, there may be an extension service in your region or county that can help you find farm-fresh foods or harvest festivals or can answer your questions about food preservation or gardening.

Word of mouth. Is there a chicken farmer in the house? Ask around. Ask. Ask. Ask. Ask neighbors, ask your local city council member, ask the chamber of commerce, ask the little old lady next door who was born in your town. You might find a farm and strike up an interesting conversation to boot. Get used to piping up. You're going to need assertiveness skills to find out whether your food is sustainable. If you're shy, don't worry. There are resources to help you get your questions answered.

The printed word. You can't swing a cat (not that you'd want to) these days without hitting an article or a book about local food. Some farmers and food producers advertise in newspapers. Regional magazines also often carry information about "agritourism," so check the calendar section for information on seasonal festivals, farmers markets, or farm tours. There are also "Edible" magazines springing up, from Austin, Texas, to Missoula, Montana, that focus on local food.

All of them are run by a parent company, Edible Communities (www.ediblecommunities.com).

Drive around. I know—driving burns fossil fuels. Who says you can't carpool or ride a bike? In any case, head for the countryside. Drive slowly because you'll not only want to watch for chickens crossing the road but also for signs posted at the entrance to a farm, advertising fresh eggs, honey, sweet corn—you name it. Bring your appetite, curiosity, and sense of adventure. Also bring your manners—see "Farm Etiquette for Urbanites" later in this chapter.

Think seasonally. Even in chilly New England, where summers are short, I go to local farms in every season. In spring, I go to a sugarhouse for the first batch of maple syrup. Summer, of course, means weekly trips to my CSA farm (for more information about Community Supported Agriculture, see "Ask an Expert: CSA Farmer Elizabeth Keen," also later in this chapter) and to farmers markets. Autumn's bounty gives me an even wider choice: I go to farms to stock up on pastured (grass-fed) meat for the winter and visit other U-pick farms to pick apples and pumpkins or to take my kids through a corn maze. In winter I visit yet a different farm for my Christmas tree. (For more seasonal thinking and eating, thumb on over to Chapter 7.)

WHAT IF IT'S LOCAL BUT NOT SUSTAINABLE?

A food may be local, but that doesn't mean I'm going to buy it. Why not? Because it might not be sustainable—that is, grown or produced in a way that supports the ongoing health of the land, animals, farmers, and eaters. Case in point: I once bought a carton of gorgeous local grapes. I didn't know how they were grown, so I called the phone number on the carton. The farmer who answered the phone was kind and almost shockingly forthcoming: "I used poisons on them," he said. I thanked him. I was nursing an infant at the time, and I did not eat his grapes. Even so, I never assume that just because something doesn't have an organic label it's not sustainable. Some farmers may not have the time or the money to achieve organic certification. Others may be in a "transitional" phase—employing organic practices but not yet certified. Some fruit and vegetable farmers also practice Integrated Pest Management (IPM), a way of controlling pests such as insects in ways that are least harmful to people and the environment. An apple farmer who practices IPM may, among other techniques, plant disease-resistant varieties to help limit the need to spray.

Speaking of produce, I will buy conventionally grown items when local and sustainable ones are unavailable. Even so, I bear in mind the heavy pesticide load on some conventionally grown fruits and veggies and avoid them altogether. The Environmental Working Group offers an excellent list of fruits and vegetables with the most and least pesticide exposure (www.foodnews.org). Not sure if that bin of apples at the farm stand is sustainable, and there's no one to ask? Here's a hint: Real produce, grown without lots of chemicals, is seldom picture perfect. Sprayed apples may look gorgeous, but the lumpy ugly ducklings are likely to be healthier—and much tastier.

PICK A PECK WITH U-PICK

Some farms offer an option called "U-pick," so wear your old jeans. This is not only a fun option for kids but also a cost-saving option for both you and the farmer. The farmer saves on harvesting costs and usually passes the savings on to you by setting a lower price per pound on what you pick. This is an especially great option for those who plan to store some food (see Chapter 4 on how to do this) because, if you're industrious or the crop yield is high, you'll come home with a lot of food. Trust me: One summer my husband, my daughter, and I came home with 31 pounds of scrumptious, ruby-red organic strawberries—after picking at a leisurely pace. The price was $1.69 per pound—a serious bargain. To find a U-pick farm, call your state agriculture department or cooperative extension office, or try the Pick Your Own website (www.pickyourown.org/index.htm).

FARM STANDS

Who says you can't get healthy food at the drive-through? You can at the farm stand! You'll find these stands seasonally along America's roadsides, and they're often in the same spot year after year. Some may be listed on your state's website. My state has an association that lists locations of farm stands selling everything from alpaca wool to pumpkins. Often, though, the best way to discover these gems is through serendipity. You never know what you might find: I've purchased roadside corn in New England, freshly roasted chiles in New Mexico, and homemade beef jerky in Colorado.

Can You Tell a Farm Is Sustainable by Looking at It?

Let's say you're truly too shy to pipe up and ask your farmer about how his or her food is grown. Aside from the absence of big drums of pesticide, is there any way to know if a farm is sustainable? Probably not, says my trusted egg farmer Sean Stanton, who farms at North Plain and Blue Hill farms. "But an unsustainable farm probably isn't going to want you there anyway." My own two cents: While I don't encourage you to play Nancy Drew and take a flashlight into the barn, I do encourage you to use your two good eyes and common sense when you go to a farm. If you are buying 100 percent pastured beef (see "grass-fed" in the Glossary), are the cattle grazing? Outside? On grass?

ASK AN EXPERT
CSA FARMER ELIZABETH KEEN

Along with her husband, Al Thorp, Elizabeth Keen operates Indian Line Farm in Egremont, Massachusetts, a community supported agriculture (CSA) farm. Under this system, one of the most innovative options for getting farm-fresh food, consumers become members of the farm by buying a share in the farmer's upcoming harvest—usually in the spring-time, when the farmer needs cash flow. In exchange for that fee, they receive a portion of the harvest weekly during the growing season. The cost of a share and what you get for it vary from farm to farm (some farms offer produce and flowers, others offer dairy and meat), as does the style of delivery. In many cases, members go to the farm and can customize their allotment of produce from that week's harvest.

The late Robyn Van En, who helped create the CSA concept in 1985, founded Indian Line Farm, one of the first CSAs in the United States. Today there are approximately 1,200 CSAs. For more information on Indian Line Farm, check out its website (www.indianlinefarm.com).

How much does a share at Indian Line Farm cost, and what do you get?

It's $550 for a regular share, which will give you enough vegetables to feed a couple or a small family. You'll get shares from June to November. It costs $175 extra for a fruit share, and the fruit comes from a variety of local farms.

How can someone reduce the cost of a share?

Becoming a working member cuts your cost by approximately $150. You give 32 hours of labor in the form of fieldwork, working at the farmers market or doing office-related work. You could also request a scholarship, and we've never turned anyone down.

What are the advantages to joining a CSA?

The greatest advantage is that you will get a fresh, eclectic assortment of food that has been harvested for you that day or one day prior.

What are the drawbacks?

In many cases, it's not convenient. It's a special trip, and your menu planning is based on what you get, and many people find that challenging. Quantity can vary according to season.

Are you an organic farm?

Not certified, but for all intents and purposes we are. We are totally transparent in terms of our growing methods.

What is the most frequent question people ask?

"What can I do with this?" or "How do I use this?"

What's the most popular item at Indian Line?

Our lettuce mix and our spinach. People can't get enough of spinach, and we always run out.

The least popular?

Fennel used to be a hard one, just because of unfamiliarity.

How's membership?

Increasing every year. We have 120 members, and we started with 10.

Why the increase?

Local food is "in" because it tastes great and people realize that they're doing a good thing.

For more information on CSAs, or to find a CSA farm, go to the Robyn Van En Center for CSA Resources website (www.csacenter.org). For information and links on finding CSAs, try the USDA's CSA page (www.nal.usda.gov/afsic/pubs/csa/csa.shtml). LocalHarvest's map also shows CSA locations (www.localharvest.org). If you prefer tangible fact finding, read the CSA primer *Sharing the Harvest* by Elizabeth Henderson and Robyn Van En (see Resources). Also be sure to find and watch the charming documentary *The Real Dirt on Farmer John* (see Resources), the true story of farmer John Peterson, whose family farm is saved when it is transformed into an organic CSA. No kidding: You'll laugh, you'll cry. For more information, go to his farm's site (www.angelicorganics.com).

FARM ETIQUETTE FOR URBANITES

Has it been a while since you've been to the farm? Have you *ever* been to a farm? No worries. Farms are fun and incredibly interesting, but their rules are way different from office rules.

- Leave your pet in the car—or, better yet, leave your pet at home. The last thing you want is to have to pay for the limp chicken that your sweet golden retriever just retrieved.
- Call first. Farmers are busy and don't work regular hours, so don't expect them to be there if you drop by unexpectedly. Ask about convenient times to stop by, or check the farm's website (yes, some farms have them) for visitor hours.
- Bring cash. Or while you're on the phone asking about hours, inquire about what kind of payment the farmer prefers. Many farmers aren't set up to take credit cards. And don't be surprised if you encounter the honor system. Many farm stands are completely unstaffed. At the farm that provides my eggs and pork, I leave money in a mason jar on top of a refrigerator.
- When in doubt, ask permission. Can you feed the chickens? Can you stroll through the tomato fields? Can your child poke around the barn? Remember, a farm is not only someone's home but also someone's livelihood. Farms also have potentially dangerous stuff around, such as barbed wire fences or heavy machinery. Don't let your kids wander unattended.
- Keep your distance from livestock. Some farms may offer a chance for dudes to mingle with live animals, but don't

touch or feed the animals (this goes for farm dogs, too)
unless otherwise instructed. Also, contain your enthusiasm;
yelling could stress the animals. Believe it or not, pigs do
not enjoy it when you shriek "su-eeeee" over and over.

- Wear sensible shoes. It almost goes without saying, but
farms may have not only dirt but also livestock poop.
Some sort of rubber boot works best, especially if it's mud
season. I once brought along a friend who didn't change
out of her purple suede boots. It was a muddy day. You
can see where this is going.

- Mind the fences. Some fences are electric. The jolt won't
kill you, but your startle response might provide secret
amusement for the farmer. "We don't mind if people
touch the fences," Dominic Palumbo of Moon in the Pond
Farm once told me dryly. "That's how we know they're
on." While we're on the subject of fences, here's a note
about gates: If you open one, close it behind you.

- Depending on the farm's protocols, you may be asked to
wash your hands or sanitize your footwear if you'll be
interacting with certain livestock. It's a good idea to wash
your hands after being around livestock. See poop, above.

- Leave your farmer stereotypes at home. The old man in
the straw hat and overalls with the pitchfork? I've never
met him. My farmers, many of them women, are young,
hip, educated, and technologically savvy. Sean Stanton,
my egg supplier, has a cell phone with a rooster ring tone.

- Speaking of cell phones, turn yours off. "It's respectful,"
says CSA farmer Elizabeth Keen. "People don't come to
the country to listen to other people talk on cell phones."

🖎 What do you do if you are approached by cattle? Roll
into a ball and cover your head. Just joking! Cows have
approached me and nothing happened. I didn't try to pet
them but moved away slowly. If you abide by the rules
of a farm and respect the fences, the likelihood that
you'll encounter a cow or some other stray livestock is
low. If you need to, push the cow away at the shoul-
der. Feel threatened? Run. A cow will generally not give
chase. Remember that bulls (male cattle, as evidenced by
testicles) can be aggressive, but also remember that not
all cattle with horns are bulls. Some breeds of cows have
horns, and all cows can be protective of calves—so stay
away from cute little cow babies even if they appear to be
alone. Chances are, momma is nearby.

FARMERS MARKETS

Ah, the farmers market—the holy place for eat-local zealots
known as locavores. But they're obviously not the only ones
going: According to the USDA, there were 4,385 farmers markets in the United States in 2007—an 18 percent increase over
2004. This popularity is no surprise. Farmers markets are not
only social, lively places, they're also the main way for carless
urbanites to get farm-fresh food. Depending on the farmers
market, you'll find much more than good produce. Many markets offer meats, dairy products, baked goods, jams and jellies,
honey, fresh flowers, and locally made crafts, such as candles or
soaps. During the summer season, farmers markets, sometimes
called green markets, tend to keep a regular schedule and occur on a certain day each week. If you're lucky, you might find

a permanent one that is open year-round. An easy way to find farmers markets is to use the USDA's web site, www.ams.usda .gov/farmersmarkets/map.html, which lists them by state.

ACCESSORIES FOR THE SUSTAINABLE SET: THINGS TO BRING TO THE FARMERS MARKET

- **Some sort of bag.** It's no fun for you (or the planet) to juggle a million little planet-polluting plastic bags, so consider washable canvas bags or cotton mesh bags. They're often sold at co-ops and health food stores, or check out Reusablebags.com. Another option is a collapsible market basket (which looks like a high-tech picnic basket). Urban shoppers often eschew bags altogether and go for a European-style trolley on wheels. If casual chic is your style, go for a *très* French straw bag. If it's high summer and you'll be buying dairy products or meats, consider bringing a reusable thermal storage bag. Ultimately, do what works and what's comfortable. My husband prefers his backpack. If you forget your bag, don't fret. Most vendors have bags on hand.
- **Kid carrier.** Farmers markets are great fun for kids, so don't forget the backpack or stroller for the little ones. Plus, you can stuff food into the carrier compartments of the stroller.
- **Cash.** Some vendors work on a cash-only basis, so be sure to hit the ATM before you go.
- **Weather-appropriate clothing.** If it's sunny, or likely to turn sunny, wear a hat. You probably don't need this tip, but I ignored it and sunburned my nose one morning. That being said, it was a small price to pay for a morning of socializing and snagging some farm-fresh sausage.

- **A leash.** If dogs are permitted at your local market, it goes without saying that you need to leash your pooch. On a personal note: Although my local farmers market is very dog friendly, I leave my dog at home. He once found a whole baguette on the ground, and ever since, he yanks me around looking for another big bread score.

- **A buddy.** Food, and all aspects of it—from acquiring it to growing, cooking, and enjoying it—has been, historically speaking, social. (Motto: Life is too short to shop alone.) If you drive to the farmers market, carpooling with a buddy or buddies will reduce your carbon footprint, in addition to alleviating boredom en route.

- **Your senses, and your good sense.** Go ahead, pick up that cantaloupe. Is it mushy? Scentless? Put it back. Choose one that smells as sweet and musky as a summer afternoon. Its flesh should give a little but not too much. My point: Examine your food and enjoy the sensual process. If the produce looks too picture perfect, be suspicious: *The fact that food comes from a farmers market doesn't guarantee that it was grown sustainably.* So, ask politely but firmly, with good eye contact:

  "Is this organic?"

  If not, "How was it grown?"

  "Were any sprays or pesticides used on the plant or in the soil?"

For a more in-depth list of questions to ask farmers and producers about meat and dairy products, check out the Sustainable Table's "tools" at www.sustainabletable.org/getinvolved/tools.

GROCERY STORES, CO-OPS, AND NATURAL FOOD STORES: FINDING FOOD OFF THE FARM

If there were ever a sign that local food is coming into its own, it's the fact that you may be able to find local products at your average grocery store. That having been said, mega-stores are probably not (at least not yet) the best place to find local and sustainable fare. For this reason, you're likely better off trying a regional grocery store chain that may be more responsive to your questions or requests. Look for such stores in the phone book, through your local chamber of commerce, or on the Internet.

Many grocery stores are starting to label products that are local, organic, or "transitional" (this last term indicates that the farmer is in the process of receiving his or her organic certification). Because there are so many labels on food these days, you'll have to be a savvy shopper to decipher which labels to trust. Did you know that "free-range" chickens don't necessarily go outside? (They must only have access to outdoors.) Or that "natural" products can contain artificial ingredients? (I tend to roll my eyes when I see that term.) Or that "hormone-free" is misleading in some cases? (Because it's illegal to give hormones to hogs or poultry in the United States, a hormone-free chicken label states the obvious. It's more important to know how the chicken was raised and what it ate.) For more information on what food labels mean, go to the Consumer Reports GreenerChoices eco-labels center website (www.greenerchoices .org/eco-labels). Be sure to click on the virtual kitchen, a quick visual way to learn about eco-labels.

Health food stores (sometimes referred to as "natural food

stores"), which often sell vitamins and other supplements as well as food, are another option for finding local food. *Caveat emptor:* Compared to a big-box store, the food in these stores is expensive. Think quality, not quantity—and then take every advantage of sales, coupons, and buying in bulk (I buy grains, nuts, seeds, and even sugar from bulk bins). An even more cost-effective option for bulk buying (for organic but not necessarily local food) is a buying club (also known as a pre-order co-op). The concept is simple: A group of people pool their money to buy food in bulk at wholesale prices from cooperative warehouses or retail distributors.

For fresh local food, try a co-op store, which looks like a conventional grocery store. (Please note: You do not have to be a member to shop at a co-op grocery store!) At mine, the Berkshire Coop, I paid a fee to become a member, which not only allows me to have a voice in how things are run but also lets me buy certain items—chlorine-free diapers and eco dish detergent—in bulk. Members also have the option of working there to further reduce their costs. My co-op, like most, helps customers learn about sustainable and healthy food through newsletters, meetings, and events such as a harvest festival. It supports local farmers and local food, from fresh seasonal produce to eggs and meat to locally made bread and cheese. To find a co-op near you, try the LocalHarvest database (www .localharvest.org) or check the Coop Directory Service (www .coopdirectory.org), which also has information about starting your own co-op. Another resource for starting your own is the National Cooperative Business Association (www.ncba.coop), which offers a "food club buying package" for $24.

Last, don't forget natural foods chain stores. At Whole Foods, which merged with Wild Oats a while back, you can find clearly labeled local foods in season. Whole Foods also hired its first full-time "forager," who forages not for wild food but for local farmers and artisan food producers to supply Whole Foods stores. (Hello? Can you say *dream job?*) Whole Foods also walks the talk in terms of supporting foods through its Local Producer Loan Program, which makes $10 million available annually for low-interest loans to small, local producers. *Tip:* Don't only look for local produce; look for local dairy products, meats, grains, or even specialty items such as honeys or jams. To find a natural foods chain store near you, try the Yellow Pages or the Internet.

RESTAURANTS

Fun as it is, all of this farm-going is tiring, and at the end of a long week you might want a meal someone else prepared. But where can you get a local pale ale to go with that grass-fed burger with local cheddar? Try searching the database for member restaurants on the Chefs Collaborative website (www .chefscollaborative.org). The collaborative is a national network of 2,500 chefs and food professionals who promote sustainable and local food. If you still can't find a restaurant that serves up healthy local fare, Melissa Korgut, executive director of Chefs Collaborative, suggests that you go to your favorite restaurant and ask questions such as "Is there anything local on the menu?" The Sustainable Table provides a list of questions to ask restaurant managers or, for the very shy, cards you can leave behind to show your support of sustainable food (www .sustainabletable.org/getinvolved/tools/).

Another source for restaurants that serve sustainable local fare is Heritage Foods USA, which offers humanely raised, traceable, heritage-breed turkey and other products. Heritage Foods USA is the sales and marketing arm of Slow Food USA, a nonprofit organization dedicated to celebrating regional cuisines and products. Its website offers an interesting but somewhat limited list of restaurants and stores that support heritage foods (www.heritagefoodsusa.com/friends/restaurants.html).

If you're on the road, "real food" (as opposed to commercially or conventionally packaged "food") advocate Sherri Brooks Vinton advises that you go for the local eatery, such as a family-owned pizza place, to keep dollars in the community and get a taste of the regional cuisine. Vinton is the co-author of the much-recommended book *The Real Food Revival: Aisle by Aisle, Morsel by Morsel.* For other tips about how to find real food while on the road, check out her website's Sustainable Solutions (www.sherribrooksvinton.com/ss2.htm).

CAN SEAFOOD BE LOCAL AND SUSTAINABLE?

"It can't be local for everybody," says Melissa Korgut. "But we ask people to take into consideration sustainable fishing practices so that they can preserve fish for generations to come."

Many of the world's fish stocks are now seriously threatened thanks to unsustainable fishing practices. For posterity's sake, Chefs Collaborative developed the Seafood Solutions program, which helps chefs and restaurants purchase and serve sustainably sourced finfish and shellfish. Want to find sustainable seafood choices at a store near you? The Marine Stewardship Council (www.msc.org), a nonprofit organization devoted to making sure there will "always be plenty more fish in the sea," can help you find a store that carries types of fish that aren't from exhausted stocks. Depleted stocks, of course, aren't the only problem with fish. Mercury from industrial pollution falls from the air into bodies of water and ends up in fish. Because some species of fish and shellfish contain high levels of mercury that may harm unborn babies and little kids, the FDA and the EPA recommend that women of childbearing age, pregnant women, nursing mothers, and young children avoid them and eat seafoods that are lower in mercury. As of press time, the USDA does not have organic standards for fish. To track your fish dinner's sustainability *and* its mercury levels, use a seafood "watch list" provided by marine advocacy groups, such as the Blue Ocean Institute or the Monterey Bay Aquarium, that you tuck into your wallet or post on your refrigerator.

Should you buy farmed fish? Well, that's another kettle of fish, but I'll give you my very brief opinion here: I avoid farmed salmon, which are often fed antibiotics, are lower in omega-3 fatty acids, and have a weird texture to boot. But that's not all: According to the Sierra Club, farm-raised salmon have been found to have significantly higher concentrations of PCBs, dioxin, and other cancer-causing contaminants than wild salmon. For yet more compelling reasons to avoid farmed salmon, read more about the topic on the Sierra Club's website: www.sierraclub.org/e-files/wild_salmon.asp.

ASK AN EXPERT
TOD MURPHY OF THE FARMERS DINER

Imagine you've been on the road for a couple of hours. Your whole family is weary and hungry, and the kids are whiny. You see the bright lights of fast-food restaurant row . . . and you pass them by. Instead, you pull into the parking lot of a classic-looking diner. The logo on its sign is simple: a draft horse pulling a farmer on an old-fashioned plow. On the menu you find affordable, traditional comfort food—burgers, fries, milkshakes—all made from fresh local foods and supplied by local farmers. Is this a hunger-induced mirage? Not if you're in Quechee Village, Vermont, home of The Farmers Diner (www .farmersdiner.com). Full disclosure: My husband and I were so taken by the diner's fresh food and even-fresher concept that we decided to put our money where our mouths are and become very small-time investors in the diner.

What's the average price of a lunch?

$9.50, $11.50 with a beverage.

What's the most popular thing on the menu?

Two eggs, home fries, bacon, and toast. Cheeseburgers at lunch. Hush puppies as an appetizer.

What's your favorite?

Cranberry yogurt parfait—it's all local, mostly organic, looks great, and tastes wonderful. I get excited by the idea of Vermont cranberries.

What's the most frequent question customers ask?

"Are you going to open a Farmers Diner [wherever they are from]?"

Who is your average customer?

You, your kids, the guy who painted your house, the bus driver in your town, the folks who double the population there in the summer.

Does a local grass-fed burger taste different from an average burger?

Not just local grass-fed. Locally *killed* and *butchered* beef tastes different from organic beef killed, cut up, packaged, and shipped 1,500 miles. Of course, grass-fed tastes different, flesh tastes different based on diet. Milk—raw—tastes different based on what is in bloom in the pasture throughout the year. That is part of the pleasure of being in a place, and of a place, and awake to life in a place.

Why isn't your whipped cream white?

Real cream is yellowish, hence yellow butter, and more so in early spring and summer.

Are you able to get Vermont tomatoes in January?

Almost. They stop December 7th and start again March 15th. I am searching for another supplier to fill in the three- to four-month off-season.

What's the most popular song on the jukebox?

The most popular song of jukeboxdom in the U.S. is Patsy Cline singing Willie Nelson's "Crazy."

THE POWER OF THE TOQUE

Chefs, it is no surprise, have played a leading role in the sustainable food movement because of their authority on the subject of food. In fact, much of today's local food movement is credited to chef Alice Waters, who founded the landmark restaurant Chez Panisse in Berkeley, California, in 1971. Her philosophy? Serve high-quality seasonal food supplied by a network of sustainably minded local farmers and ranchers. Much more than just a "star chef," Waters is an advocate and activist for local and sustainable food, farmers markets, and revolutionizing America's school lunch program. The Chez Panisse Foundation supports programs such as Berkeley's Edible Schoolyard, which provides fresh food for public schools (see the section "School Gardens" in Chapter 2). Waters's latest cookbook is *The Art of Simple Food: Notes, Lessons, and Recipes from a Delicious Revolution.*

GOING LOCAL WITHOUT GOING LOCO

The journey of a thousand miles. . . . Oh, you know the rest. Here's how to begin your local food journey without feeling overwhelmed.

- **Start slowly.** Try replacing one item in your diet—say, apples—with a local one. Or earmark a small portion of your food budget for local foods. If you set goals that are too unrealistic ("I'll eat within twenty miles of my home for an entire year with no exceptions!"), you might not only burn out but be hungry and cranky—or, worse yet, nutritionally deficient.

- **Start in the summertime, when the livin' is easy.** It's much easier to find local foods at the height of growing season.
- **Get social!** Form a supper club, start a blog, or join an online community such as The Hundred Mile Diet (www.100milediet.org). Join a CSA as part of a group, such as a church group. Look for local food events such as pig roasts and clambakes. Take a buddy to the farmers market, sip Fair Trade coffee, and shop together.
- **Find an expert.** Take a class on cheesemaking, get a guide for learning about wild edibles, or find a friend who knows how to make fruit leather.
- **Involve the kids.** From growing tomatoes to picking apples and making pies, kids can be a part of finding and enjoying local foods. My daughter loves going to the coffee roaster to see the big Willy Wonka-ish coffee-roasting machine. My infant son gets toted by backpack to farms and farmers markets.
- **Be gentle with thyself and set realistic goals.** For those items I can't find locally, such as coffee and tea, I opt for "Fair Trade" products, which means that the farmers, often disadvantaged ones in developing countries, receive fair prices for their products. If I can't buy something sustainable and local, I'll try to go for organic. If I can't buy something local or organic or Fair Trade, well, I've given things my best shot, and I don't lose sleep over it. And sometimes I just want a Snickers. For me, local eating is a choice, not a mandate. A monotonous diet is not only

a recipe for failure (ask any dieter) but antithetical to our need for nutritional variety to stay healthy. Citrus fruit in winter is a blessed thing that I try not to take for granted.

Make a game of it. Are you the up-for-a-challenge type? Organizations such as the Ecotrust of Portland, Oregon, provide guidelines and scorecards (www.eatlocal.net). Locavore blogging groups, such as Eat Local Challenge (www.eatlocalchallenge.com), can offer support. I ate locally (within 50 miles of my house) for two months one summer and had a lot of fun. Don't be afraid to draft your own rules, ones that work for your family. Eco-author Bill McKibben coined the term "Marco Polo exemption" for the seven-month local eating stint in Vermont that he wrote about for *Gourmet* magazine. McKibben allowed cooking items a thirteenth-century explorer would have brought along, such as salt, pepper, yeast, and so forth. Best-selling author Barbara Kingsolver, who wrote about her year of local eating in *Animal, Vegetable, Miracle*, let her family members choose a few items they couldn't live without, such as chocolate or coffee. (These are sometimes called "wild cards.") I never gave up coffee, but I did find a company that roasted its organic coffee locally.

🌿 **Alter your expectations.** As I have mentioned, sometimes produce raised without pesticides isn't pretty. Don't be shocked if you occasionally find bugs—yes, bugs—in local produce. Got your first pound of grass-fed beef? It tastes a little different from grain-fed beef, and it needs to be cooked more gently. Farm-fresh eggs may come in different colors (blues, greens, and browns) because egg color depends on the breed of chicken. Other thoughts for the uninitiated: Farms smell farm-y. Gardens are dirty. Cooking a meal from scratch takes more time than heating up a Lean Cuisine (ick) frozen dinner. An organic carrot is more expensive than a regular one. It's not always easy or comfortable to pipe up and ask questions about what the bleep is in your food. But take a look at your child's face, your waistline, or a gorgeous stretch of healthy farmland and tell me it's not worth it.

🌿 **Meet other locavores online.** Check out blogs or post comments on websites. (I like the posts by farmer/chef Tom Philpott on www.grist.org.) You can also look for friends on social networking websites, such as MySpace.

Sustainable in the City: Portland, Oregon

Don't think sustainable and local food can only be found in the countryside. Urban areas offer local food options, ranging from farmers markets and community gardens to top-notch restaurants that highlight local, seasonal foods.

One of the shining examples of a local food city is Portland, Oregon, which, for a smallish city (pop. 533,427), packs a wallop when it comes to sustainable and local. For starters, you can garden here almost year-round. "Though Californians might complain about the rain, it is good for growing—and not just moss," says Oregon native Tara Miner. "Chanterelle mushrooms on the Coast are worth more than gold, and people are literally willing to kill for them." Because Portland happens to be only about 60 miles west of the Hood River Valley, one of the best fruit-growing regions in the United States, it can offer much more than fungi: luscious apples, cherries, and pears. Of course, Portland's culinary calling card is its native salmon and steelhead, which, once filleted, go nicely with a glass of pinot noir, for which the region is also known. If you are more the beer type, you can find any style of handcrafted brew at one of Portland's 28 breweries.

If you don't want to forage at one of the metro area's 34 farmers markets, you can shop at grocery stores so lovely that you'll want to move in. (Oh, and you can find local food there, too.) "Portland has the best grocery store I have ever experienced," says Miner, referring to New Seasons Markets, a local chain of nine stores. "You can purchase local food and goods in an aesthetically pleasing, well-planned-out store, chock full of friendly and knowledgeable employees who actually enjoy helping customers." For more information about Portland and its remarkable foodshed, search out the small but wonderful spiral-bound book *Portland's Bounty: A Guide to Eating Locally and Seasonally in the Greater Portland and Vancouver Areas,* published by the Ecumenical Ministries of Oregon's Interfaith Network for Earth Concerns. Although it is currently out of print, you can find copies of it on Amazon.com.

Chapter 2

GROWING YOUR OWN: SAVE MONEY, REDUCE STRESS, AND MAKE TASTIER MEALS THROUGH GARDENING

aybe you can't find local food no matter how hard you try. Or perhaps you want to take your "local and sustainable" goal a bit further and save some money. (Have you, perchance, compared the price of basil seeds against the tiny and costly package of basil at your market?) Or maybe you want to get some exercise and spend time with your kids outdoors while you're at it. . . .

Well, grab a trowel and get busy!

But before we start, let me put something on the table, so to speak: I am not advocating, or even suggesting, that you become a farmer or that you feed your family entirely from the garden. Although farming can be wildly appealing on many levels, it's incredibly hard work. As a cautionary tale, read Manny Howard's hilarious account of creating and eating from a backyard subsistence farm in Brooklyn, New York ("My Empire of Dirt," *New York Magazine*, September 17, 2007). I won't spoil the whole story, but I will let on that Howard spent $11,000, had limited success keeping rabbits alive, and cut off a finger. He lost 29 pounds and nearly his marriage, too. "Unless you really know what you're doing," he wrote, "raising [food] is miserable, soul-crushing work. Eating food fresh from the farm, on the other hand, is delightful."

Okay, so not everyone's soul gets crushed by farm work, and I'm thankful that some folks love it enough to provide my food. Even so, I feel compelled to spend time in the garden growing some food of my own. It's gratifying to know that even a black-thumber like me can make food out of dirt. (I once worked for a landscape company pulling weeds. The only plant I was allowed to touch was dandelion because, despite repeated instruction, I couldn't identify any other plants.) I also cannot grow herbs indoors, no matter how hard I try, even with a plant light. Consequently, you won't see any exhortation in this chapter about how easy it is to grow windowsill herbs. What you will find are general tips for growing something sustainable to eat.

- **Increase the fun factor: Involve kids.** My all-time favorite edible plant for kids is nasturtiums. They're colorful and fast growing, and they have gorgeous, peppery blooms. Some of my favorite kids' gardening ideas come from the sweet book *Sunflower Houses: A Book for Children and Their Grown-Ups* by Sharon Lovejoy. Among Lovejoy's suggestions for kids' gardens is a "mini-trough" garden planted with miniature and dwarf varieties of vegetables such as Little Sweetheart sweet peas. Garden centers are also excellent places for fun kid ideas, as are websites such as www.kidsgardening.org.
- **Use a local garden center.** I find that local garden centers, unlike many big retailers that happen to sell plants, offer healthier, well-grown plants and more personal service, which is important because I tend to ask lots of questions. There are other benefits, too. "Local garden centers tend to be family owned with a strong connection to the community," says Greg Ward, whose family

business is Ward's Nursery, my local source for plants and horticultural advice. "They are more likely to get involved and help support that community. That connection makes it possible for you to affect what that garden center has to offer simply by asking."

- **Lose the lawn.** Okay, not entirely. A lawn is a great place to toss a Frisbee to your dog. But the average lawn is treated with toxic weed killers, and it hogs both water and your precious weekend hours. Consider ditching the chemicals and providing some space for an edible garden, or planting edible landscaping such as fruit or nut trees or a patch of edible berries. To kill off some grass, don't use chemicals. Smother a small patch with an old blanket or a piece of cardboard (not newspaper, because certain inks can contain heavy metals). This can take several months, so consider starting the process in the fall for your spring garden. Then improve that patch of bald soil by adding organic compost (most nurseries will deliver it), or make your own (see "Ask an Expert: Composting Guru Karl Warkomski," in this chapter). Because my own lawn contained unacceptable amounts of lead, my husband and I had to take somewhat radical measures to make a vegetable garden. We had part of our driveway removed. Now we not only have a garden, we have less asphalt to shovel off in the winter.

- **Consider a raised garden bed.** Digging and bending is hard work for those of us (ahem) with aching backs and can make gardening impossible for the elderly or disabled. A raised garden bed (sometimes known as an RGB) means less bending. It also produces better yields because you can better control water and (organic) fertilizer. Plus, you don't compress your garden beds by walking on them, and airy soil is happy soil, which makes productive plants. You create a raised garden bed by building a frame from wood, stones, or bricks and filling it with soil so that it is higher than the surrounding ground (it should be approximately 12 inches deep for vegetables). Or, you can buy an RGB kit that you assemble; just add compost/soil and you're ready to plant. Look for RGB kits at garden centers or on online gardening sites.

- **Start at the very beginning**. The best place to start an organic garden is with organic seeds. Seeds of Change (www.seedsofchange.com) offers 100 percent certified organic seeds for edibles, flowers, and cover crops (plants that are grown specifically to nourish the soil after a harvest). Legumes, for instance, add nitrogen to the soil. When cover crops such as clover are turned into the soil, they are known as "green manure."

- **Test your soil.** It may be of low quality and require amendments. More worrisome, it may contain serious pollutants, such as heavy metals. My soil test revealed lead in the garden around my 100-year-old house. Lead in the soil isn't uncommon around older homes because leaded exterior paint was often removed by scraping or sandblasting, which caused the contaminated paint dust to fall to the ground. Call your cooperative extension office for soil testing services. Test results will give you the dirt (sorry, this pun was hard to resist) on your soil's pH, its proportion of organic matter, and any nutrients needed to balance it. If soil amendments or fertilizers are recommended to improve your dirt, ask your extension agent or local garden center for sustainable/organic alternatives.

🌿 **Know thy neighbor.** Take a look around. Does your neighbor have a flawless, deep-green, velvety lawn? Be suspicious, very suspicious. He or she might be using toxic chemicals to maintain that turf. Several common pesticides used in lawn care are classified by the EPA as probable or possible carcinogens. Some of these chemicals are associated with a variety of other health problems, including liver and kidney damage, damage to the nervous and endocrine systems, and severe skin irritation and respiratory distress. (Children are particularly susceptible to these risks.) If you are concerned that your neighbor's chemicals are leaking into your yard, take a deep breath, bake a batch of muffins, and knock on your neighbor's door. Calmly explain your concerns and ask what kind of chemicals he or she applied. (You may get some help here: Although there is no federal law requiring pesticide notification, some communities have chemical registers and notification laws.)

🌿 **Bone up on organic pest control.** Did you know that marigolds, often planted with vegetables, attract beneficial insects such as lacewings, ladybugs, and parasitic wasps? They also contain compounds that are toxic to parasitic nematodes—worms that damage plants. In addition to promoting "companion plants" (for instance, many gardeners swear that insect pests such as nematodes hate garlic, so it is often planted near roses), many nurseries carry nontoxic pest control products, such as a spray-on chrysanthemum extract. *Caveat emptor:* Even nontoxic pest control has its drawbacks. I once dropped a bottle of deer repellent in my kitchen and it squirted everywhere. Among its non-toxic ingredients were rotten eggs. You can guess how my kitchen smelled . . . for a week. If good homemade remedies (the Internet is chock full of recipes for sprays based on garlic, hot pepper, or soap) fail to deter pests, head to your local garden center. Many sell predatory insects such as ladybugs. (We sometimes keep ours in the refrigerator—an excellent conversation starter for houseguests.) Don't forget about chemical-free barri-ers—for instance, you can install netting to deter birds from munching your berries.

Go native. Talk about local! Try planting things that grew in your region prior to European settlement. Because they are adapted to your climate and your soil, "natives" are hardy once established, need less maintenance, and often require little watering. Nonedible natives can be great for attracting birds and butterflies, and native edibles will attract all sorts of animals, including humans. Accord-ing to Project Native, my local source for native plants circa 1491, my native edibles include elderberries (good for wine and jam), wild strawberries, and mountain mint. For information about native plants in your area, check out Wild Ones (www.for-wild.org), an organization with 50 chapters in 12 states devoted to advocating for native plants and biodiversity.

- **Choose heirloom varieties.** Who wouldn't be intrigued by a Jelly Melon cucumber or a Moon & Stars watermelon? Unlike today's hybrid plants, which are created by large seed companies and will not reproduce true, heirloom plants come from seeds that have been passed down from generation to generation. Heirloom fruits and veggies can offer great flavor, fun colors, and cool histories that will thrill kids and adults alike. Start by requesting a catalog from an heirloom seed company. My favorite is Seed Savers Exchange (www.seedsavers.org). Among the seeds my family ordered for the garden this year are Green Zebra tomatoes, Detroit Dark Red beets, Tennis Ball lettuce, French Breakfast radishes, Five-Color Silverbeet Swiss chard, and Jolly Jester marigolds.

- **Hire a backyard farmer.** Do you have the yard but not the time? Are you lucky enough to live in the Portland, Oregon, area? If so, you can hire Your Backyard Farmer (www.yourbackyardfarmer.com). For a fee, farmers will plant and maintain an organic garden in your backyard, then leave a weekly harvest basket on your doorstep, delivered by draft horse. (Just kidding about the draft horse part.)

- **Consult a master.** Not everyone is as lucky as I am: My mother-in-law (MIL) arrives with a bottle of wine, pruners, and seedlings from her vast garden. I'd be lost without her gardening advice. If your MIL isn't so helpful (hold your tongue, now), contact your state cooperative extension office and ask to be connected with a "Master Gardener." In exchange for their training, Master Gardeners share their time and expertise. In my neck of the woods in western Massachusetts, an independent Master Gardeners association answers questions and hosts clinics and training sessions. Other places to find experts: gardening clubs, horticultural societies, nurseries, garden centers, and your neighbors (I've never met a fellow gardener who wasn't eager to talk about what he or she was growing). Don't forget about TV shows—my favorite is the PBS show *The Victory Garden*—and gardening radio shows, some of which have a call-in component.

〜 **Get potted!** Do you live on a small city lot or in an apartment? Wee patios, small balconies, and even rooftops can host potted edible plants. Container gardening has many benefits: If the weather changes, you can bring your plants indoors; if you move, you can bring your entire garden with you. Also, no weeding! (Sigh. Makes a small-town girl want to move to the big city.) I am not an urban gardener, but I am a huge fan of potted dwarf citrus. Though these tiny trees will not supply my vitamin C for the winter, the mere whiff of their blooms on a gray February day feeds my soul. For great container gardening tips, try the website www.containergardeningtips.com, and for urban gardening help in general, try—you guessed it—www.urbangardeninghelp.com.

〜 **Conserve water.** Rain barrels collect rain from the rooftop that would normally just gush out of your downspouts onto the ground. Soaker hoses and drip irrigation use less water than conventional sprinklers or spray hoses that lose water to evaporation. Water only in the mornings, when the temperature is cooler and there's less evaporation. Don't water at night; if the plants are damp all night, you increase the risk of fostering molds or fungi. Lastly, use an organic mulch to retain soil moisture.

- **Get a gizmo.** Maybe. If you have a yen for garden-grown greens but limited space, time, or daylight hours, there are high-tech options: Garden centers and online retailers sell mini-greenhouses, hydroponic (water-immersed) growing kits, indoor plant lights, and aeroponic (dirt-free) gardening growing systems. Keep an eye on sustainability, cost, energy efficiency, and ease of use. You don't want one more thing in the appliance graveyard (where the bread machine has gone to die).

- **When all else fails, plant tomatoes.** "Starting a garden is really a daunting task," says Jon Piasecki, a landscape architect friend who has a vast organic vegetable garden. "If I were to pick one bulletproof plant that will succeed and bring lots of tasty food, I would pick cherry tomatoes." Cherry tomatoes, he explains, need two things: at least six hours of sun a day and a little bit of water if they start to wilt. "At this point I have a huge vegetable garden," he continues, "but my cherry tomatoes are always right near the kitchen door, so when the basil bolts, the lettuce dries out, the corn is stunted, or the potato bugs are defoliating the potato plants, I still go into my house past the gorgeous cherry tomatoes, and all is well."

THINK VICTORY!

Not so long ago, gardening was patriotic. During World War II, as many as 20 million families planted "victory gardens" (aka "war gardens"). Through boosterish campaigns ("Our food is fighting!" and "Dig for victory!"), the government encouraged people to grow food in their backyards or rooftop gardens. This eased the pressure on the food supply when food staples were rationed. My grandmother helped feed her family of eleven (phew!) with a vegetable garden, a few fruit trees, and a grape arbor (for jelly, of course). What's that? You don't think back-yard veggie gardens will make a comeback in the era of plasma screen televisions and iPods? Knitting and bell-bottoms are popular again, so anything is possible.

COMMUNITY GARDENS

Let's face it: Chores like weeding are more fun when you have company. So why not beautify your neighborhood, grow some sustainable food, and have fun weeding with new friends by joining a community garden? The American Community Gardening Association (ACGA) defines a community garden broadly: any piece of land gardened by a group of people. These can be school gardens, hospital gardens, church gardens, neighborhood gardens, or even prison gardens. Some of these are "market gardens" that sell what is grown. According to the ACGA, there are an estimated 18,000 community gardens in the United States and Canada. To find one near you, search the ACGA database by clicking on the map on its website (www .communitygarden.org). If you don't have a community garden nearby, consider starting one; the ACGA's website has a "Ten Tips Series" that includes helpful hints.

ASK AN EXPERT
COMPOSTING GURU KARL WARKOMSKI

Karl Warkomski was the first Green Party member elected to serve as a councilman and mayor in Orange County, California, and co-founded the website composters.com. He now works for a company that makes the Biopod, a composter that uses black soldier fly larvae to make super-speedy compost.

Why compost?

Composting is the best way to divert all of your green waste—food scraps, grass clippings, paper, yard waste—from the landfill and transform it into free, nutritious soil you can use in your garden.

Is composting a messy, stinky process?

If it's contained in a tidy compost bin, your pile of decomposition can be an out-of-sight, out-of-mind process. As long as you don't let water pool at the base of the unit, and you make certain there are aeration holes throughout, you should mitigate bad odors and have finished compost in four to eight months. Using a pile turner to stir your pile every two to four weeks will help speed up decay.

What should go into the compost that will be used for an edible garden?

You can add everything except pet waste [because of pathogen issues], pharmaceuticals [chemical concerns], bones [long decay cycle], and glossy print [heavy metals].

How can I keep animals out of my composter? What about bugs or flies?

The best way to keep critters, including pets, out of your tempting pile is to limit it to plant materials. Meat, dairy, and poultry products are irresistible to hungry foragers. All insects and small microfauna are beneficial to compost piles, so you should encourage them. If you have a filth fly problem, simply bury your kitchen scraps under some shredded newspaper or leaves and the flies will have a difficult time reproducing.

What's the best kind of bin if you're short on space?

The one with the smallest footprint is the best unit for compact gardens—look for bins that are taller, to maximize vertical space.

What's the best bin if you're short on cash? (Do you need a bin at all? Can you make one?)

Prefab compost bins are quite affordable, and can start at under $30. Some sort of a bin is recommended in order to neatly contain the pile. If you are a creative soul by nature, then you might want to construct one out of recycled materials you can find locally.

What if I think composters are, well . . . ugly?

Ethan Allen does not yet manufacture a Queen Anne compost bin. You can go with wood units made out of cedar or white pine that are quite attractive. You can also get a typical wooden screen that you would normally use to hide garbage bins. The third option would be to get somebody creative to use spray paint to really spiff up the bin with cool colors and designs.

How long does it take to make compost? Is there any way to speed up the process?

Normal backyard composting is a relatively slow process and can range from four to eight months, but it can take longer if you have lots of material that has a low surface-to-volume ratio. The more you can chop up the waste, the faster it will decompose. Keep the unit constantly moist and cover the pile to retain heat, and you should have favorable results in under a year.

How do you know if you've made a good batch of compost?

It will be friable and black, with a rich, healthy aroma.

What's the most common error people make when making compost?

The biggest problem is trying to overengineer the process—you don't need to follow specified ratios or add accelerators. Just like food rotting in the refrigerator, composting will happen without much oversight or intervention.

How should I use my compost?

Use it to amend your vegetable garden, perennial beds, or shrubbery. Fresh compost makes a great gift for a plant lover.

How can I get the kids involved?

Make it interesting and assign them exclusive responsibilities, so they can feel a sense of ownership in the process. Have them be in charge of throwing in the kitchen scraps or yard waste, and encourage them to monitor the decomposition rate over the months. Have them identify some of the beneficial inhabitants, like black soldier fly larvae and worms.

In the Zone

It seems as though you can't pick up a gardening book, magazine, or seed catalog without seeing a reference to "hardiness zones." You can find yours on the USDA's Plant Hardiness Zone Map (www.usna.usda.gov /Hardzone/ushzmap.html). Created in 1960 and updated in 1990, this map uses minimum temperatures to determine which plants will "winter over" (read: survive) in your area. Sounds simple, except that global warming has already turned up the temperature in many parts of the country. Luckily, the Arbor Day Foundation updated the USDA's map again in 2006, using the very latest weather station data. Much as I suspected, my ever-warming region of western Massachusetts jumped a zone, from 5 to 6. If it's getting hot in your neck of the woods, also consider using the American Horticultural

Society's Planet Heat Zone Map, the zones of which indicate the average number of days each year on which a given region experiences "heat days" with temperatures over 86°F. To get the map, go to ahs.org/publications /heat_zone_map.htm.

Does your zone designation still seem inaccurate? Blame it on your "microclimate"—which might be noticeably different from the one on the map if you live at a higher elevation, near an urban area (concrete jungle), or close to a body of water. Or you might even notice that certain parts of your garden are hotter or cooler than others—next to a light-colored south-facing wall, or at the bottom of a slope where cold air drains downward. If that's the case, don't despair. Ask your green-thumb neighbors or your local garden center how to make the most of your special circumstances.

Hardiness Zones Map

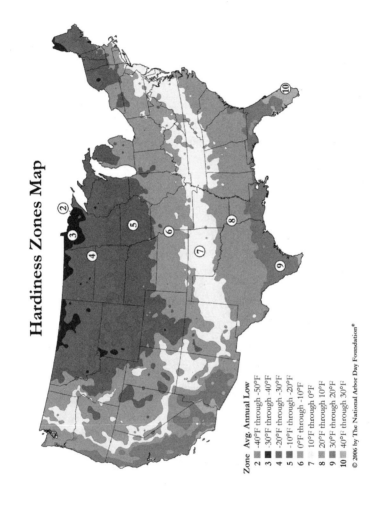

Zone Avg. Annual Low
2   -40°F through -50°F
3   -30°F through -40°F
4   -20°F through -30°F
5   -10°F through -20°F
6   0°F through -10°F
7   10°F through 0°F
8   20°F through 10°F
9   30°F through 20°F
10 40°F through 30°F

© 2006 by The National Arbor Day Foundation®

SCHOOL GARDENS

You probably know the bad news: Childhood diabetes and obesity rates are climbing, while at the same time our school cafeterias, which have devolved into "reheating centers," are serving up heaping portions of commodity transfats, GMO-laced "frankenfoods," pesticides, and high-fructose corn syrup (known to its many foes as HFCS). My own school-food memories can be summed up with the key phrases "mystery meat," "Tater Tots," and "fruit cocktail." All of this "food" is not only contributing to rising rates of diabetes and obesity in kids but might be affecting their wee brains, too. Pediatric expert Dr. Alan Greene, in a series of essays for the Center for Ecoliteracy (www.ecoliteracy. org/publications/rsl/alan_greene.html), points to solid science showing that kids need balanced diets and whole foods for optimal brain function. That leads me to this really deep thought: Shouldn't a learning environment serve brain food?

Now for the good news: There are superheroes, a whisk in one hand and a garden trowel in the other, working toward revolutionizing the nation's public school lunch program. At the heart of many of these programs lies a school garden.

The prototype program is the Edible Schoolyard, which operates on the campus of the Martin Luther King Jr. Middle School in Berkeley, California. In 1994, a conversation between Berkeley chef Alice Waters and then-principal Neil Smith put the wheels in motion. Two years later, an empty lot at MLK Jr. Middle School was transformed into an organic garden, and an abandoned cafeteria became a kitchen. Today, the school's curriculum is coordinated with the students' activities in the now-thriving one-acre garden and a new kitchen in a renovated bungalow.

The lucky sixth, seventh, and eighth graders participate in the entire process of sustainable food production, from seed to table. Teachers and volunteers work with students to plant flowers (which are set on tables for meals) and, of course, fruits and vegetables that are harvested and turned into super-fresh seasonal dishes.

But the learning experience doesn't end with the meal. Following the principles of ecology, students use food scraps to create compost for the garden, thus completing the cycle of nature. According to the Chez Panisse Foundation, which supports the program, more than 3,000 students have graduated from the Edible Schoolyard. It receives over 1,000 national and international visitors a year and has inspired several similar programs across the country. To learn more and to find resources for creating a similar program at your child's school, go the Edible Schoolyard's website, www.edibleschoolyard.org.

If your child's school can't have its own garden, that doesn't mean that fresh, nutritious food isn't an option. For information on incorporating sustainable and local food into school lunch programs, see the following sources.

🍃 **A good book** about the problem and its solutions: *Lunch Lessons: Changing the Way We Feed Our Children*, by Ann Cooper and Lisa Holmes. Cooper, the "renegade lunch lady," is the chef who is transforming meals from frozen to fresh at the Berkeley Unified School System's 16 California schools. Her program, funded by the Chez Panisse Foundation, will undoubtedly serve as a model for other schools across America.

- **A sexy Brit with a cause.** Check out the DVD *Jamie's School Dinners*. Okay, not only is celebrity chef Jamie Oliver cute (gush, gush), but he managed to charm, cajole, and cuss his way to changing the school lunch program in England. If he can do it, so can we! Go to his website, read his manifesto about school food, and even see him in a fat suit (www.jamieoliver.com/schooldinners).

- **The documentary "Two Angry Moms."** Filmmaker Amy Kalafa and gal pal Susan Rubin show how to channel that protective momma-bear anger into advocating for real food at school. To buy their music video, host a screening of their documentary, or find the nearest screening of the film near you, go to www.angrymoms.org.

- **Farm to School programs.** Good news: According to farmtoschool.org, as of early 2008 an estimated 1,117 programs in 34 states connect 10,943 schools with local farms. Even better news: There are more in the planning stages. For more information or to find a program near you, check out the website's map (www.farmtoschool.org).

- **Farm to College programs.** Fresh food isn't just for little ones; colleges and universities are getting on board. In 2007, the University of Massachusetts purchased 20 percent of its produce from area farms and opened a farmers market on its campus. The FoodRoutes Network has teamed up with the Community Food Security Coalition (CFSC) and the National Campaign for Sustainable Agriculture to create a set of resources for students interested in starting a farm-to-college program (www .foodroutes.org/farmtocollege.jsp).

TIP: If you can't beat 'em, pack 'em. What to do while you're waiting for change to happen in your school? Pack lunch. Does it take more time? Sure, but tossing a piece of fresh local fruit into a lunchbox (a lead- and vinyl-free one, of course) takes no time at all. Plus, you know where your apples come from. Can you say that about goopy fruit cocktail? My saintly husband packs my daughter's lunch every day. His secret weapon: a 10-ounce stainless steel Nissan "food jar," a compact thermos that will keep soups and leftovers hot for hours.

GARDENING THROUGH THE SEASONS

Eating fresh food from your garden is a bit like drinking good coffee: Once you've had it, you can never go back to drinking freeze-dried instant or to eating tasteless fare from the frozen food aisle. But what if your growing season is woefully short? (When I lived in a Colorado mountain town at an altitude of 8,750 feet, we joked that the seasons were composed of "July, August, and winter.") If you're like most gardeners (and me), your idea of gardening is to plant enthusiastically in the spring and then burn out completely over the summer. By fall the garden is a neglected brown wasteland, and you're in the supermarket reaching for a bagged salad that sparks fear of a potential E. coli recall in your heart. But with the following tips you can garden through the seasons with less effort and more fresh food.

Spring
Start your seedlings indoors a month or two before the date of your last frost. It's a fun project to do with kids, and

a bit of mood booster for those of us who start to feel seasonally affected during February. To grow sturdier seedlings, use grow lights. You may have to move seedlings into bigger pots as they grow, so keep an assortment of different-size ones on hand. (Here's an opportunity to use up those cottage cheese and yogurt containers in the recycle bin. Poke holes in the bottom for drainage and use organic potting soil from the local garden center.) Move the seedlings to bigger containers when they sprout two leaves. Before you can plant them outside, you'll need to "harden off" your seedlings (acclimate them to the outdoors and prevent shock) by putting them in a protected area, such as under a row cover, for one or two days. No luck with homegrown seedlings? Ask around at local nurseries for organic "starts" or small plants. Better luck next year.

Don't get frosted! If you're going to plant early, keep an eye on the weather and watch for early frosts. You can also cover up your precious plants by using cloches (you can make a reasonable substitute for those pricey glass bell jars by cutting the bottoms off two-liter plastic jugs), floating row covers (available at nurseries), or a cold frame, which is like a big picture frame you plant under. Some gardeners build cold frames out of hay bales, topped with glass or transparent plastic. Maximize sun and warmth by sloping the lid toward the south. I'm designing a cold frame using old windows that we saved rather than discarded after a home remodeling project. Note: Don't use toxic materials, such as railroad ties, which can contain creosote. Ditto for pressure-treated lumber, which can leak chemicals such as arsenic into the soil.

Dear Garden: Today I woke up and the sun was shining ...

A garden journal is a fun family project that can allow you to pin down a fussy microclimate by recording all sorts of details, such as your daily temperatures and frost dates. My own garden journal is more like a scrapbook: It's a three-ring notebook with pockets that contain garden maps, my daughter's garden art, notes about successes and failures, seed catalogs, articles, and wish lists. This year I plan to add digital photos.

Want to peek into the past and someone else's journal? In *The Garden and Farm Books of Thomas Jefferson*, edited by Robert C. Baron, you can read Jefferson's comments about the potatoes of Monticello and his letters to George Washington! If you're not as prolific a record-keeper as our polymathic third president, check out the garden journals sold at many bookstores, as well as others that are free online in PDF format. For those Virgo-ish gardeners who like lavish detail when it comes to garden journals, Seeds of Change (www .seedsofchange.com) offers both print and online versions of its GardenCycle journal, in which you can record all sorts of gardening information from temperature to wind direction.

GREEN CONUNDRUM: PLASTIC IN THE GARDEN

So, you're planting in a sustainable, chemical-free way, yet your four-season garden seems to be begging for a lot of plastic, from seed cups to row covers. Plastic is handy and ubiquitous. But some plastics contain nasty chemicals, and all plastics take a lot of energy to create (not to mention a lot of petroleum) and a loooooooong time to break down in landfills.

To use or not to use?

I say use plastic if:

- **It won't be directly in the soil for a long time and it's an okay kind of plastic.** Here's a quick rule of green thumb: Don't put any plastic into your soil that you wouldn't allow in your baby's mouth. Why not? According to the Institute for Agriculture and Trade Policy (IATP), the "use of plastics in cooking and food storage can carry health risks, especially when hormone-disrupting chemicals from some plastics leach into food and beverages." Remember, soil is food for plants and plants are food for you. To choose a healthier plastic, whether it be for gardening, food storage, or your garden gnome, look at the recycling number on the container and remember this little ditty (courtesy of IATP): "With your food use 4, 5, 1, and 2. All the rest aren't good for you." For information, check out the IATP's Smart Guide to Smart Plastics (www .iatp.org/foodandhealth).

- **You can reuse it many times,** as in the case of a polyethylene row cover. For rigorous thinking about the energy that goes into making plastic for the garden and why reusing it still makes sense, see "Appendix C: Do We Really Need Plastic?" in Eliot Coleman's *The Four-Season Harvest: Organic Vegetables from Your Home Garden All Year Long.* The bottom line: Until a better alternative comes along, some reusable plastics are still a good bet, energywise.

- **It's not PVC.** Many do-it-yourself season-extender projects, such as hoop tunnels (very big row covers), call for PVC pipe. PVC, or polyvinyl chloride, is one plastic you should avoid for sure. According to Grist.org's advice maven, Umbra Fisk, the manufacture, use, and disposal of PVC involves dioxin, phthalates, lead, and other stuff that can cause cancer, endocrine disruption, endometriosis, birth defects, respiratory problems, and immune system damage. On that note, if you are going to water your edible garden with a hose, or let your kids or pets drink from a hose, get a "drinking water safe" hose that doesn't contain either PVC or lead. I get my Flexeel hoses, which are made in the USA and constructed from polyurethane, from Nature's Tapestry (www.naturestapestry.com). Fellow gardeners, repeat after Umbra: "No PVC for me," and "No vinyl, that's final." For more advice from Umbra, go to www.grist.org.

Summer

- **Keep sowing.** One trick to keep your garden going longer is to do "succession planting," or planting at intervals so that new plants replace mature ones. Some veggies, such as lettuce, can be planted every couple of weeks!

〜 **Keep weeding.** One of the biggest problems in gardening
(believe me, I know) is running out of steam, and there's
nothing as energy zapping as weeding. Keep it at, because
weeding is like cleaning up as you cook: There's nothing
worse than a kitchen full of dirty pans or a garden full of
weeds when you're tired. Don't forget to use a high-quality mulch (such as shredded leaves from your trees), which
will keep the weeds down and decompose into something
yummy for your soil.

〜 **Plant veggies for fall.** Depending on where you live, sow
cool-weather-loving plants that you can harvest in the fall.
Spinach and broccoli are two good bets.*Here's the tricky
part:*You might have to shade these plants from too much
sun! Use row covers or even other plants to provide shade.

〜 **Keep picking.** Don't let your zucchini get as big as goril-
las. They don't taste as good, and once the plant starts
producing seed it will stop producing fruit. If you have too
many zukes, give some to your neighbors or a local food
pantry that accepts fresh foods.

Fall

〜 **Grow cool-weather-loving greens under your cold
frame, if your area's climate allows.** Begin planting as
the weather cools, and choose plants that love "sweater
weather," such as broccoli, cabbage, lettuce, chard,
and beets. For advice on cold frames, what vegetables
to plant, and why ducks are fun to have around, I like
Eliot Coleman's book *The Four-Season Harvest.* Food for

thought: Coleman grows stuff all year long in Maine—
without heated greenhouses.

🌱 **Save cash and precious genes by saving seeds.** Collect seeds from your celebrity plants (the robust, tasty,
and gorgeous ones) because you'll want to pass on those
genetic traits. Speaking of genetics, harvest seeds from
plants grown from "open pollination" plants, not hybrids.
Hybrid seeds do not breed "true," but revert to the original plant parents, not the variety you planted. Do you still
have seed packets left over? Take a tip from seed banks,
which store seeds in a cold place, and put your leftover
seed packets in a jar in the refrigerator. This will help you
get a few more seasons out of them. For books, supplies,
and more information about seed saving, try the Seed
Savers Exchange website, www.seedsavers.org.

Winter

🌱 Enjoy the food you've stored. (We'll look at this topic in
more detail in Chapter 4.) Cozy up with some seed catalogs
and plan your spring garden. Update your garden journal.

🌱 If you live in a cold climate, don't let your garden be
lifeless: Hang some bird feeders. Make a fuss over your
houseplants.

🌱 Depending on where you live, you might still be plucking
salads from your cold frame.

🌱 Go ahead and try your hand at an indoor herb garden.
Just don't take advice from me, aka The Handmaiden of
Basil Death.

🌱 Make your "fireside read" a book about sustainable food.

Lou's Canon: One Woman's Must-Read Local & Sustainable Food Reading List

≫ *Animal, Vegetable, Miracle: A Year of Food Life* by Barbara Kingsolver with Steven L. Hopp and Camille Kingsolver.

As you'd expect, this account of eating locally by a best-selling author is well written as well as honest, insightful, warm, funny, and informative . . . with recipes to boot! Warning: After reading it, you may want to move to Virginia (near Kingsolver, ideally) and take up small-scale farming. Extra-neato: The book is a family affair, with sections written by her husband and her college-age daughter.

≫ *Coming Home to Eat: The Pleasures and Politics of Local Foods* by Gary Paul Nabhan

No local-food reading list would be complete without this groundbreaking book. Nabhan is Ed Abbey meets Anthony Bourdain meets sensitive brainy New Age guy! This is deep ecology and deep food. Be prepared: Nabhan eats roadkill—and you'll love him for it. Who is he? Scientist. Author. Lecturer. Doctor. MacArthur Foundation fellow. A leading expert in the conservation of native plant agriculture.

≫ *Plenty: One Man, One Woman and A Raucous Year of Eating Locally* by Alisa Smith and J. B. MacKinnon

After reading this book, you might not be so enthusiastic about eating within 100 miles of home, especially if your home is a remote cabin in Canada. At least I wasn't. You will, however, have a profound respect for Smith and MacKinnon (www.100milediet.org), whose dedication, raw honesty, and writing are a pleasure and an inspiration. Extra-juicy morsels: This author duo were not only brave enough to write about how hard their year was in terms of local food; they also detailed the pressures it put on their relationship. Thankfully, theirs was a happy, and tasty, ending.

≫ *The Real Food Revival: Aisle by Aisle, Morsel by Morsel* by Sherri Brooks Vinton and Ann Clark Espuelas

Although this book is not technically a local-food book, it is an indispensable primer to everything that's wrong with industrial food and to finding what's right and real and good and nourishing and delicious. Plus it has the hat trick I look for in great food books: recipes, resources, and good writing.

The Omnivore's Dilemma: A Natural History of Four Meals by Michael Pollan

I didn't want this book to end. Pollan, our national food systems pundit, doesn't just think about what he eats; he explores things deeply and brainily. Astonishingly, all of this research doesn't ruin his, or the reader's, appetite. Spoiler alert: Our bookish hero learns to hunt and kills a wild pig, and he's a better man for it. Don't stop here: His other books, such as *The Botany of Desire*, are wonderful too, and his essays in the *New York Times* are well worth looking up. His latest book is *In Defense of Food: An Eater's Manifesto*. Pollan will be the man remembered for saying that, when it comes to American food, the emperor has no clothes.

OPEN-FACED BEET SANDWICH

Okay, people, I know what you're thinking: *Oh goody! Beets! What's the second prize? Brussels sprouts?* Trust me, this sandwich is a winner. It's a much-modified version of a recipe I found in *Gourmet* magazine years ago. I like it because it's made from two easy-to-grow-in-cool-weather ingredients that gardeners often have on hand: arugula (sometimes known as rocket) and beets. Roasted beets, earthy and slightly sweet, contrast nicely with the peppery flavor of arugula and the tanginess of chèvre. Even my fussy six-year-old likes this one. Go ahead and serve it with iced tea dolled up with mint from the garden.

1 teaspoon Dijon mustard

1 teaspoon balsamic vinegar, organic if possible

A dash of salt and pepper

3 tablespoons high-quality olive oil, organic if possible

3 or 4 small roasted beets (preferably left over from dinner the night before), thinly sliced into discs

8 slices bread (I use a crusty *boule*-style bread; my favorite is "country wheat")

6 ounces goat cheese (my local one, Monterey Chèvre, comes in a thyme and basil flavor, and I use that)

About 24 arugula leaves (arugula, which is like catnip to me, works best here, but you can substitute other zingy greens such as dandelion greens and watercress)

Half a small red onion, sliced into very thin rings (use more or less depending on how much you like raw onion or whether you have a date later)

Yield: 4 servings

Turn on broiler. Whisk together mustard, vinegar, salt, and pepper, then drizzle in 2 tablespoons of the olive oil. Toss beets in this vinaigrette and set aside.

Brush one side of the bread with some of the remaining olive oil and toast under the broiler until firm and golden, for one minute or less (you don't want to blacken the edges!). Remove from oven, turn bread over, and smoosh goat cheese onto bread. Broil until cheese is hot and slightly golden, one minute or less.

Remove beets from vinaigrette. Top each piece of chèvre-topped bread with beets, then arugula, and then onions. Drizzle any remaining vinaigrette over the sandwiches, which can be served either open-faced or closed.

VERY MINTY ICED TEA

The next time you make iced tea, sweeten it with a batch of intensely minty simple syrup made with garden spearmint. (Gardeners, please note: Mint will spread rapidly, seeking world dominance, so consider growing it in a container.) This syrup can be used for mint juleps as well as for iced tea. For a less intense version, strain out mint leaves as soon as the syrup has cooled.

1 cup sugar
1 cup water
A generous handful of chopped mint leaves
Unflavored iced tea
Fresh mint sprigs, for garnish

Heat sugar and water in a nonreactive saucepan until sugar dissolves and mixture is clear. Add chopped mint leaves and cook a minute or two longer. Remove from heat and let cool completely. Cover and place in fridge for at least three hours. Strain out the mint leaves and store syrup in the fridge in a glass container for up to one week.

Add 1 tablespoon (or to taste) of syrup to each tall glass of iced tea. Garnish drinks with fresh mint.

Chapter 3
FORAGING: ENJOY THE GREAT OUTDOORS AND EAT FOR FREE

*V*alderi, valdera! A snackpack on your back!

For many Americans, the taste of a berry fresh from a wild bramble is the equivalent of Proust's madeleine: One bite can bring you back to the sun-drenched summers of your childhood. It's not just the distinctive taste of a wild berry that is so simple and profound, but also the special feeling that comes with eating something nature has provided. "The tragedy of the grocery store is the amnesia that robs us of our gratitude," says Hank Lentfer, an avid forager who lives in Gustavus, Alaska. "When you go out and gather something, the food is received as a gift." Lentfer provides roughly half of his family's food by foraging, hunting, and fishing. Berrying can be a fruitful (ahem) affair for Lentfer and his wife, Anya, whom he refers to as "The Berry Queen." During a good year the couple can gather up to 50 gallons of berries. "That's a lot of work," he admits. "Weeks and weeks of work."

Although not many of us have the desire or the stamina that will let us collect at that scale (let alone the natural bounty of Alaska), foraging for wild edibles—plants you can eat that are not cultivated or propagated by humans—can be another enjoyable way to add truly local food to your diet. It's hard to believe that foraging, once a common and pleasurable activity for Americans (just ask your parents or grandparents), is now as exotic as, say, trekking in Bhutan. Trust me: Foraging for wild edibles is not only fun and tasty but—get this—free!

I am an enthusiastic forager. In Colorado, I was so bowled over by the intense flavor of high-mountain strawberries that I once spent an entire hike looking at my feet rather than the glorious scenery around me. And, feeling like a pith-helmeted explorer, I once set out with a group of mycologists to find meaty *Boletus edulis* mushrooms (aka porcini) that we later sautéed in butter. In New Mexico, with the help of locals (twelfth-generation New Mexicans, actually), I ate fresh piñon nuts, rich and resinous, knocked from the trees and then roasted in their cones over an open fire. Here in New England, I nosh on wild raspberries, teaberries (*Gaultheria procumbens,* also known as wintergreen), and fox grapes (*Vitis labrusca*), and I have snacked on fruit leather made from the berries of autumn olive (*Eleagnus umbellata*), aka autumnberry, an invasive shrub with edible berries that happens to be rich in the antioxidant lycopene. Thanks to the help of an expert foraging guide, Russ Cohen (see "Ask an Expert: Wild Edibles Foraging Guide Russ Cohen," later in this chapter), I can identify spicy sorrel, and I now know how and where to find wild hickory nuts and black walnuts, should the squirrely urge hit me. My husband keeps an eye on a secret wild blackberry patch in the woods, and he takes my daughter there on hazy August days. If the bears haven't been there first, they return with stained fingers and buckets full of tart-sweet treasure.

Besides being an enthusiastic forager, I'm also a cautious one. Before you plan on raiding nature's larder, bear the following safety tips in mind.

- **Rule #1:** Unless you are absolutely sure it's edible, don't eat it.
- **Rule #2:** See Rule #1.

🍃 **Get a guidebook.** There are many, ranging from general to specific. My favorite is the 1962 foraging classic *Stalking the Wild Asparagus* by Euell Gibbons. Are you old enough to remember Euell? He's not just the guy who stumped for Grape Nuts cereal in the 1970s. His foraging career started in his teens, when he kept his family from starving by foraging. He later lived entirely on a foraging diet for several years. His book—part guidebook, part cookbook, part memoir—is a charming place to start if you're new to foraging. Beyond that, be sure to check with your local library or bookseller for guidebooks specific to your area.

🍃 **Know what you're doing.** Foraging for some plants (wild raspberries, for example) may be straightforward, but other wild edibles can be tricky, to say the least. Some edible wild mushrooms have poisonous lookalikes that fruit at the same altitude, at the same time of year, and sometimes even in the same patch! According to Russ Cohen, many poisonous plants taste bad, but he is careful to point out that this rule does not apply to mushrooms; many deadly ones taste just fine. As noted, when I forage for mushrooms I go with a mycologist.

🍃 **Get a guide.** Try your favorite Internet search engine, and don't think that just because you live in the city you're out of foraging luck. The country's most famous forager, "Wildman" Steve Brill, conducts foraging tours in none other than Central Park. In fact, he was once arrested for foraging there, but that's another story. For information about Brill's foraging tours, TV clips, recipes, or how to book him for a children's birthday party, check out his website (www.wildmanstevebrill.com).

∾ **Take a class.** Check with local colleges and universities, nature centers, and conservation groups to find a course on foraging for wild edibles. Wilderness and outdoor survival schools also offer foraging classes, but be aware that the emphasis there may be on challenging yourself rather than on enjoyment.

∾ **If you are trying a wild food for the first time, eat only a small amount.** It's possible that you will have a reaction, perhaps an allergic one, to a new food.

∾ **Avoid picking in areas that are polluted.** Cohen advises against noshing near busy roads, manicured-and-therefore-possibly-pesticide-laden landscapes (such as golf courses), industrial sites, and areas that have heavy human and dog traffic (common sense will probably tell you that it's best not to forage in a dog park).

∾ **Foraging with kids can be fun and rewarding, but take extra precautions.** Make sure children are old enough to understand safety rules, such as this one: **Never** pick and eat something unless and until a grown-up approves of it! And keep all plants away from babies who are, obviously, too little to obey safety rules.

∾ **You don't know for sure what killed Bambi's mother.** Was it really hunters, or did she eat a toxic mushroom?

"Just because an animal has taken a bite out of something doesn't mean it's safe," Cohen advised a group of amateur foragers (including me). "Who knows? Maybe that animal died a horrible death."

In addition to playing it safe, always use your best manners when it comes to both Mother Earth and her children. That is to say . . . .

Be a good steward of the land. Cohen advises that you pick from a good-size patch of plants and leave enough behind to ensure the plant's survival. An exception to that rule: invasive species. (The bane of the Pacific Northwest is the Himalayan blackberry. In the Northeast it's Japanese knotweed. Then of course there's kudzu, "the vine that ate the South.") When it comes to edible invasive plants, pick and eat as much as you can (with the help of a guide and a guidebook), but take care not to further spread the plant in the process.

Use your manners. If you are going to forage on private land, contact the landowner and ask for permission. If you are going to forage on public land, do the same. Contact a ranger if you are going to forage in public parks; rules on public lands vary. When in doubt, ask. I'm sure your neighbor will be delighted when you tell her you'd like to cart off some of her dandelions. (For a curried dandelion recipe, go to Wildman Steve Brill's website.)

From the Acorn, a Mighty Bread

All acorns are edible. Produced by oak trees all over the world, acorns are high in protein and fat. They are an important food source for many animals, and for thousands of years the portable, easily harvested, nutritious nuts were crucial to the survival of *Homo sapiens* as well. Though some acorns are yummier than others (you have to taste them to tell), all acorns are bitter because they contain tannic acid. Soaking them is the easiest technique for reducing the bitterness. (Native Americans often soaked their acorn caches in streams.) Once the bitterness is removed, acorns are sort of like tofu—versatile because they are bland. In his book *Oak: The Frame of Civilization*, William Bryant Logan, who has eaten his fair share of acorns, describes making pancakes with acorn flour. He writes, "The acorns added no flavor, but they did add that odd feeling of being very quickly filled and satisfied. Five hours later, I still felt that way." Want to nosh from your old oak tree? The cookbook *Acorns and Eat 'em* by Suellen Ocean is available as a free download at the California Oak Foundation website, www.californiaoaks.org/html/reference.html.

ASK AN EXPERT
WILD EDIBLES FORAGING GUIDE RUSS COHEN

Russ Cohen, a rivers advocate for the Massachusetts Department of Fish and Game, is in his fourth decade of leading foraging walks in New England. He received a "Heritage Hero" award from the Essex National Heritage Commission in 2006 for his foraging writing and programs. He is also the author of *Wild Plants I Have Known . . . and Eaten*. For more information on Cohen and his schedule of foraging walks, go to his website, users.rcn.com/eatwild/sched.htm.

Why forage?

Foraging is a great way to appreciate and connect with nature in a visceral, tangible way. I do it for the atavistic thrill of being outdoors and nibbling on the landscape. It's a celebration—a happy, wonderful thing. It is communion.

Is foraging safe?

It's like anything else: Do it with awareness and common sense.

Where can someone find a foraging guide?

Internet searches. The internet is making it easier to find a guide or a class about what's in your area. There are a lot of good books. But even with a good book it's best to complement it in the field with instruction by someone who knows what he or she is doing. I tell people that I didn't learn this stuff by popping stuff into my mouth and seeing what happens.

What's one thing a forager can do to tread lightly on the land?

Eating weeds and invasive species is guilt-free foraging. There are many common weeds that are delicious, such as dandelions, and you can pick and eat all you want without any adverse impact.

What is the "sixth sense" that foragers talk about?

You begin to get little clues in the landscape that a wild edible you are interested in will pop up. For example, sometimes you will see fruit pits or nutshells on the ground. Look up—you might see a tree laden with fruits or nuts right above you.

How much of your own diet is composed of wild edibles?

At most, ten percent—that will vary seasonally. It's a fun way to complement a conventional diet. Ninety percent of the time I eat like everyone else.

Is it difficult to cook with wild foods?

I'm not a purist. When I make a pie with wild ingredients I don't use yak butter as shortening. With a little bit of tweaking, a normal recipe will accommodate a wild ingredient.

What's your favorite wild food?

It depends on what day it is when you ask me that question because with foraging you have to pay attention to the season. This time of year I'm picking autumn olives, so they're at the top of my list right now.

ARE YOU BERRYING IN BEAR COUNTRY?

Bears and other animals adore plump, juicy berries, too, so if you are berrying among bruins, make some noise. Bears don't want to be surprised, and in most cases they'll run away fast if you make a racket. You can yell the old classic bear greeting of "HEY BEAR," or my favorite shout, "HEY BOO-BOO! LET'S GO GET US SOME PIC-A-NIC BASKETS!" Or just sing. My husband, who once collected grizzly scat for researchers in Montana (his idea of fun), said it was not uncommon to hear groups of hikers belting out "She'll Be Comin' Round the Mountain" in bear country. Hank Lentfer, who gathers strawberries, blueberries, red huckleberries, nagoonberries, and high-bush cranberries in Alaska (where bears tend to be, shall we say, large), doesn't make noise unless he's in particularly thick brush. "It's one of the cool things about berry picking—the bears are there at the same time of year for the same reason," he says. "You keep an eye on each other and you keep a distance." If your eyesight isn't so good, or if you can't carry a tune in addition to your backpack, you can always wear bear bells. Which, of course, brings me to this joke: How can you tell black bear scat from grizzly scat? The grizzly scat has little bells in it.

SUPER SECRET STASH: TRICKS FORAGERS USE TO KEEP THEIR FAVORITE BERRY PATCH A SECRET

Maybe they just never learned to share as kids. Or maybe the tendency of foragers to hoard their edible booty harkens back to the days when feast-or-famine was the rule for humankind. Whatever the case, some foragers have been known to:

1. Park their cars far away from the picking site.

2. Point their cars in the opposite direction of where they are walking.

3. Be vague when asked about where they are picking. The question "Where did you find those nagoonberries?" might be answered with "Somewhere west of Japan" or even with a look of feigned bewilderment. "If you even *ask* where the nagoonberry patch is, it means you are new to town," says Lentfer. "It's sort of like asking somebody why their baby is so ugly. It's just one of those questions you don't go to."

4. Keep odd hours. The early bird gets the worm . . . and the juicy berries.

5. Use X to mark the spot. Foragers know the lay of the land and keep track, mentally or through notes, maps, and landmarks, of where and when to return year after year. Did you find a patch of tasty wild asparagus growing along a fence on a dusty country road? You might want to plug the coordinates into your little black book. Or Google Earth, if you're inclined that way.

6. Be good about sharing after all. "Nagoons are so precious, such a gift," says Lentfer. "There's no way they can't be shared. There's no way you'd make a pie and not invite the neighbors."

RUSS COHEN'S JUNEBERRY MUFFINS

Juneberry (*Amelanchier canadensis* and related species), also known as shadbush or serviceberry, is a common shrub throughout the United States. According to Cohen, Native Americans used the berries in pemmican (their version of Power Bars), which was made from dried berries, dried meat, nuts, and melted fat. If that's not your cup of wild herb tea, try this muffin recipe. Cohen says it works equally well with fresh, frozen, or dried Juneberries and that you can also substitute blueberries, raspberries, or cranberries. These muffins are wonderful: sweet, chewy, and dense—but not in that dreadful bran-muffiny way!

1 cup rolled oats (regular, not instant)

1 cup buttermilk or sour milk (to make sour milk, mix 1 cup whole milk with 1 tablespoon lemon juice or vinegar)

1 cup flour

1 teaspoon baking powder

$^1/_2$ teaspoon baking soda

$^1/_2$ teaspoon salt

$^3/_4$ cup brown sugar, lightly packed (it's okay to substitute maple sugar)

1 egg, beaten

$^1/_4$ cup butter, melted

1 to $1^1/_2$ cups Juneberries (fresh, frozen, or dried; if using dried berries, soak in hot fruit juice just to cover until softened and then discard extra liquid; frozen fruit need not be completely thawed before use)

Yield: 12 standard-size muffins

Combine rolled oats and buttermilk or sour milk in a small bowl and let stand for approximately 20 minutes to allow oats to soften. Preheat oven to 400°F. Grease the muffin tins.

Combine flour, baking powder, baking soda, salt, and brown sugar and stir well. Mix together beaten egg and melted butter; combine with the oat/milk mixture and mix well. Add oat mixture all at once to the dry ingredients and stir just until all ingredients are moistened (do not overmix). Fold in Juneberries.

Fill the muffin tins three-quarters full. Bake for 17 to 22 minutes, until muffin tops turn golden brown.

From *Wild Plants I Have Known . . . and Eaten* by Russ Cohen

Chapter 4
UNCANNILY SIMPLE: FOOD PRESERVATION FOR MERE MORTALS

ere's the thing about fresh, tasty, nutritious food: You're going to want it to stay that way. Aside from keeping it tasty, you want to prevent it from spoiling and making you sick. Not to bore you with details, but the truth is that, for the most part, fresh foods start to lose their texture, nutrients, and flavor once they are harvested. Light, heat, moisture, and even their own enzymes start to break the food down. This means that you're going to have to pay a little extra attention to storage, because a fresh berry, unlike a box of Pop-Tarts, won't last until the next ice age. And speaking of ice, I am a big fan of easy storage methods like freezing, so don't think you have to spend your autumn nights stooped over the stove putting up dilly beans. Make your mother-in-law do this.

There are lots of methods for preserving foods—curing, smoking, pickling—but for the average person these methods are too time consuming and involved, so I'm not including them here. (I'm also not including irradiation as a food preservation method, for obvious reasons.) You are also *not* going to find canning tips here, for the same reasons, plus the fact that canning spooks this home-ec flunker because of its potential for fatally poisoning your loved ones.

Before I move on to the basics of food storage, here are some sources of information, comfort, and inspiration when it comes to squirreling away fresh food.

- **Good books.** My favorites are *Preserving Summer's Bounty: A Quick and Easy Guide to Freezing, Canning, Preserving, and Drying What You Grow*, published by Rodale

Books, and *The Busy Person's Guide to Preserving Food: Easy Step-by-Step Instructions for Freezing, Drying and Canning* by Janet Chadwick.

- **The National Center for Home Food Preservation.** Created by the Cooperative State Research, Education and Extension Service and the USDA, this organization has an easy-to use site (uga.edu/nchfp/index.html) that addresses most food preservation methods. You can watch slide shows and videos, sign up for a self-study course, order print publications, get seasonal tips, or just bone up on or troubleshoot your favorite preservation method.

- **Find an expert.** Call your local cooperative extension office. They may be able to connect you with a Master Preserver, who, like a Master Gardener, volunteers in return for extensive education. Some extension offices staff seasonal food-preservation hotlines.

- **Enlist a friend.** Many hands make fast work. Do you have a friend, an aunt, or a neighbor who makes a mean apricot jam? Ask him or her to show you how in return for dinner. You could also make it a potluck party and invite others. Be sure to thank your food-preserving friend by sending him or her home with some of the fruits of your collective labor. My personal advice: Find, and marry, a partner who enjoys food storage. My husband has the energy and inclinations of a caffeinated homesteader. Lucky me! But if your partner would rather watch the World Series, don't fret. Thanks to modern conveniences such as blenders and freezers, food preservation has never been easier.

🥄 **Share the harvest—and the gear.** Don't feel as if you need to run out and buy a bunch of appliances. My husband and I do the bulk of our storage with a food processor, a bag sealer, and a big freezer. Rather than buy a food dehydrator, I borrow one from a friend who in turn occasionally borrows stuff from me. Don't have a food processor? Use your blender. Don't know anyone with a food dehydrator? Use your oven or the good old-fashioned sun. Appliances are nifty and they save time; but they're not worth the credit-card debt; they use a bunch of electricity; and, let's face it, they're one more thing to clean.

FREEZING: WHY I ADORE THE COLD

Friends call me Snow Miser! Okay, not really, but I love freezing stuff. In fact, I am so into freezing that I finally splurged for a big Energy Star–rated chest freezer. (Energy Star appliances meet the energy efficiency guidelines set by the EPA and the U.S. Department of Energy.) This big white box allows me to feed my family easy-to-prepare meals without all the creepy additives of store-bought frozen foods. Here are some freezing tips I've learned along the way.

🥄 **Keep your freezer about two-thirds full.** Air needs to circulate around frozen foods. An under- or over-packed freezer doesn't work as well. A nice trick: We keep plastic 2-gallon jugs of frozen water in our chest freezer. This not only helps keep our freezer fuller when supplies are running low, but, should the power go out in a thunderstorm, the jugs will help maintain the freezer's temperature, which should be 0°F.

- **Freeze fresh foods quickly.** Pick or choose fruits and vegetables at their peak ripeness. If you're not going to eat them in a day or two, preserve them in some way to make the most of their wonderful texture, flavors, and vitamins. To maximize flavor and all those nutrients, don't let those fresh-picked berries molder on your counter. Get them into the freezer as soon as you can because the natural enzymes in produce will cause them to spoil.

- **To freeze veggies:** Wash and chop them. Then blanch them (cook them *al dente* in a large pot of lightly salted boiling water, tasting them for doneness—they should be firm. Then drain and dunk them in a quick ice bath to stop them from cooking further. If you cook them too long they will be mushy!) After blanching, put your veggies into freezer bags or freezer-safe plastic containers. Leave room for expansion (about a half-inch of "head space" or "head room"). Blanched veggies will keep in the freezer for up to nine months. According to *Preserving Summer's Bounty*, veggies that you usually eat raw, such as lettuce, are least suited for the freezer. Don't believe it? Go ahead and try freezing some salad.

- **To freeze fruit:** Some fruits, such as apples, will discolor when sliced. To prevent this, soak chopped fruit in acidulated water ($1/4$ teaspoon of ascorbic acid per quart of water). Sugar, or even honey, is often added to fruit that will be frozen to help retain its pretty color and to improve its taste. You can sprinkle sugar on the fruit or, alternatively, freeze it in a simple syrup (mix equal parts sugar and water and bring to a boil until the sugar dissolves and the mixture is clear).

TIP: We spread our berries out onto cookie sheets and put them in the freezer. After they're frozen, we put them in vacuum sealer bags and then use them for smoothies, baked goods, and sauces. Fruit will keep in the freezer for up to a year. We find this method works especially well for blueberries and raspberries but not so well for strawberries, which tend to get mushy, so we prefer to purée them or cook them into compotes.

Frequently asked questions: "Can I freeze eggs?" (Not in their shells.) "How long will a steak keep in the freezer?" (Six to twelve months.) "How about frozen cookie dough?" (Two months—if you have the discipline to keep it that long!) For a list of what foods to refrigerate and freeze and how long they will keep, refer to the USDA's Cold Storage chart: www.foodsafety.gov/~fsg/f01chart .html.

Keep track of what you freeze. My darling husband keeps an inventory of our frozen foods on a clipboard in our pantry. We also write the date and the contents on the front of each bag. This helps us adhere to the ole freezer rule of "First in, first out": Use the oldest stuff first if you can. Over time, frozen items may lose nutrients and texture. When items get too old to use, toss 'em. And remember, the safest way to defrost foods is in the refrigerator or the microwave, *not* on the counter. Even if you keep a log or chart, dig through your freezer's contents periodically to experience the proof of Lou's Law of

Frozen Foods: Because of fuzzy math skills, you will never
have enough frozen pork chops for company, and you will
always have too many boxes of the frozen toaster waffles
that you bought in moments of weakness.

☞ **Use a vacuum bag sealer,** which works with either fresh
or cooked foods. You cut the plastic vacuum bags (which
come in rolls) to size, depending on how much food you
have to store. Then you seal the bag with a machine that
also sucks out the excess air (while making a sound like
an angry crocodile). You can store these polyethylene
bags in the freezer.

☞ **Get strategic.** If you want high-quality weeknight meals
made with your sustainable ingredients, try a strategy
employed by busy moms everywhere: Double or even
triple your recipes and freeze a portion that can be
thawed quickly after work. Also think about recipes that
can do double duty. My husband's salsa is a good example
(see recipe later in this chapter).

☞ **A final thought about preparing produce for freezing:**
If you're going to go through all of the trouble to chop
and blanch vegetables, or peel and chop fruit and coat
it in syrup, why not just make your produce into your
favorite dishes that can be thawed for dinner? Roast your
favorite vegetables with olive oil and rosemary and freeze
them. Make huge batches of pesto in your food processor and freeze it for weekday pasta nights. Make a quick
sauce of your favorite seasonal fruit that can be used on
ice cream or drizzled onto chocolate cake.

Storage Conundrum: Plastics and Food

It's tough news to swallow, so to speak, for the Tupperware generation: There is mounting evidence that toxic chemicals from plastic containers and plastic wraps leach into food, especially when the plastic is heated. When you store in plastics, be sure to read the manufacturer's instructions. Although plastic freezer bags, like those made by Glad, are appropriate for the freezer, don't boil or microwave foods in them. Also, look for bags that are PVC-free (those made by Glad and Natural Value pass this test). Check the company's website or call its customer service department if you have questions. Storing and freezing in glass is a good option, but make sure the glass is labeled "freezer safe"; otherwise it may crack or break. For the fridge, use wax paper or butcher paper instead of cling wrap, and avoid cling wraps that contain PVC. You can also store in stainless steel. Do I use plastic for storage? I do, but this "security mom" never, ever heats foods in plastic, and I toss out old plastic containers. Then, instead of buying new plastic containers, I replace them with glass ones.

HAL'S HEIRLOOM SALSA CRUDA

In the dark heart of winter, you'll be grateful for a taste of summer that salsa will bring to your table. This basic table salsa freezes well (it can also be canned, if you're more adventurous than we are), and it's fantastically versatile. We use it on any sort of Mexican dish, from huevos rancheros to burritos, and to top fish or chicken. Often we just serve it with corn chips. It's best when made with organic heirloom tomatoes at their peak of ripeness. (We buy ours in bulk—and cheap!—from our CSA farm or from Farmer Sean, the guy who sells us our pork and eggs.) Don't skimp on flavor with pallid, underripe tomatoes. And try to mix up varieties: We combine the likes of Green Zebra (which keep their green color when they are ripe), Brandywine, and Gold Medal (a yellow tomato) to give the salsa real visual pop. Remember, the eye eats first!

3 to 6 serrano chiles
5 pounds ripe tomatoes
2 cups chopped white onion (adjust amount to taste)
$1/2$ cup minced fresh cilantro (adjust amount to taste)
$1/4$ cup olive oil
1 tablespoon kosher salt
Yield: About 2 quarts

Wearing thin waterproof gloves, cut the serrano chiles in half, trim out the seeds and white inner pith, and use as much or as little as you like. (Serrano chiles can be extremely hot.) Then finely chop them. Chop the tomatoes into roughly quarter-inch chunks. I prefer to hand-chop the tomatoes, chiles, and onions with a really sharp chef's knife (this process can be meditative, if you have the time), but you also can do it in batches in a food processor. You will get a saucier salsa using the machine—don't overprocess!

Chop or process onion and cilantro separately, and stir into chopped tomatoes and chiles. Stir in olive oil and salt, adjusting salt to taste. Serve or freeze immediately.

Why I'm a Jarhead

Q: Why is a non-canning gal like me often seen leaving the hardware store with flats of mason jars?

A: Oh, the versatile mason jar! Glorious in its unpretentious simplicity! Mason jars, also known as fruit jars, can be used for storing dry staples (nuts, legumes, grains), as vases for cut flowers, as containers for forcing bulbs (such as paperwhite narcissus, which tend to tip over), as pencil holders, for storing coin collections, or as organizers for odds and ends (from screws and nails to lipsticks, cotton balls, and sewing supplies). The tinier jars are excellent for dried spices; the taller ones can hold pasta in that upright fancy-schmancy way. I once hosted a casual summer cookout and realized that I didn't have enough matching glasses. I didn't want to create a lot of waste by using plastic or paper cups. Mason jars to the rescue! My cookie jar? A big mason jar. My child's piggy bank? Mason jar. And, speaking of cash, a cool old mason jar at a garage sale may be a collector's item. According to an eBay guide written by a jar collector, a mason jar in a rare color such as dark cobalt with an original lid could fetch more than $12,000.

DRYING

Besides freezing, the other preservation method I really like is drying (aka dehydration). It's easy to do, and dried food is easy to store (and carry, if you're camping). Plus, fewer nutrients are lost in drying than in canning.

- You can dry food outside, but this requires—big shock—sunny, dry weather. If you live in New England, as I do, you're pretty much out of luck. But even here in the moist Northeast I dry herbs by hanging them in little upside-down bouquets clothespinned to twine strung up near a window in a south-facing storage room. When the herbs look crumbly, in about two weeks, I put them into tiny mason jars. When I lived in New Mexico, where arid is the rule of thumb, I bought *ristras*—strings of chiles—and let them air-dry anywhere: on my front porch or in my living room. Go ahead and experiment! (Euell Gibbons dried blueberries in his hot attic.)

- You can also dry food in a conventional or convection oven if the oven temp can be turned down to 140°F (remember, you want to dry the food, not cook it). The bottom line: You can dry food in many ways. The section on drying in the aforementioned book *Preserving Summer's Bounty* is excellent.

- Be sure to store your dehydrated foods in labeled airtight containers. Most dried fruit or produce will keep for a couple of months at room temperature, but if you keep it cooler, say, in your unheated basement (typically about 52°F), it will keep much longer. According to *Preserving*

Summer's Bounty, dried cherries and dates stored at 52°F can be kept for 36 to 48 months!

- The good news about dehydrators is that they don't take up much space and they can do the job more quickly than the sun or a conventional oven. Also, many dehydrators have trays that allow you to make fruit leather, which is great for camping trips and lunchbox snacks.
- Rehydrate dried fruit by just barely covering it with boiling water. Soak until water is absorbed, tasting for desired texture.

ROOT-CELLARING WHEN THERE IS NO ROOT CELLAR

Thank God I don't have a root cellar. Not only do I detest my dank cellar and the way it smells, but also I'm a bit lazy. I don't relish the thought of wrapping my apples in paper or burying my carrots in sand or doing the other root-cellar-y things that industrious pioneer types do. So, if you're lazy, averse to dampness, or lacking in the cellar department, consider the following slacker methods.

If you're growing root vegetables (carrots, potatoes, turnips, parsnips) in the garden, you have the ultimate lazy person's storage option. Such veggies can be left in the ground when the weather cools—just dig or pull them before the first freeze. (Keep the ground from freezing a bit longer by covering this area of the garden with straw.) Once root veggies have been harvested, brush them off (don't wash them), cut off the stems if they have stems, and find a cool, dry, dark place if you can.

I like the refrigerator for small quantities of root vegetables. Some folks claim that potatoes become sweet in the fridge, but I don't notice it when it comes to short-term storage. The downside of using the refrigerator is that you are likely to run out of room. Luckily, root vegetables are hardy. Try your unheated garage or tool shed, but keep an eye on the temperature and don't let them freeze. Conversely, if potatoes start to sprout, temperatures are too warm. Other winter veggies that store well in the crisper compartment of your fridge? Celeriac and cabbage will keep for a month or two, maybe even longer.

A rule of thumb for spuds: Keep them in the dark (a big paper bag will do, but avoid plastic, which will encourage moisture and mold), and don't let them sprout. Toss any green ones, which could make you sick.

Hard squash and apples can be stored at room temperature on your counter for several weeks.

Garlic, onions, and shallots are fine at room temp but keep best when hung in mesh bags or open-weave baskets. If you don't have the room and do have a surplus, peel them, chop them, and freeze them. (And by all means, use your food processor!) Do you love garlic but find you're short on space? Hang a garlic braid in your kitchen: It will ward off evil spirits and free up a little premium space on your countertop, which should be saved for precious, vine-ripened, in-season tomatoes. If I were Queen of the World, putting tomatoes in the fridge (which blunts their peak flavor and makes their texture go all wonky) would be punishable by . . . having to eat them.

Yet More Handy Food Storage Tips

COOL STORAGE SUPERSTARS

These crops will keep for two to six months at cool room temperatures, and they require no processing, containers, or refrigeration. Can things get any easier than slipping a few buttercup squash under your bed, or finding a place in your closet for sweet potatoes? The sweet flavor of these two crops actually improves under good storage conditions, so you're not settling for less by storing your own. When bringing winter squash home from a farmers market, cradle them in towels to avoid accidental nicks or bruises.

Garlic benefits from cool conditions, but most varieties will keep at room temperature for several months. Do keep nuts out of the reach of hungry rodents, and freeze them after their protective shells have been removed.

Crop	Peak Season	Handling and Storage Tips
Garlic	Midsummer	Cure at 70 to 75 degrees for 2 weeks. Optimum storage conditions are 60 to 65 degrees with moderate humidity. *(May also be dried.)*
Sweet potatoes	Late summer to fall	Cure at 80 degrees for 7 to 10 days. After curing, optimum storage conditions are 55 to 60 degrees with high humidity. *(May also be frozen.)*
Unshelled nuts	Fall	Dry at 70 to 80 degrees for 4 to 10 days. Optimum storage conditions are 45 to 60 degrees with moderate humidity. *(May also be frozen.)*
Winter squash	Late summer to fall	Harvest with stub of stem attached, wipe clean. Optimum storage conditions are 45 to 55 degrees with moderate humidity. *(May also be frozen.)*

UNDERGROUND SLEEPERS

These foods will keep for two months or more under cold, moist conditions—no processing required. A root cellar is ideal, or you can bury boxes or barrels underground. (Search for "root cellar" at www.motherearthnews.com for more.) If you live in a cold climate but don't want to dig, you can store many of these crops in an unheated garage or outbuilding. In warm climates where the soil stays above 45 degrees in winter, a second refrigerator may be your best option. Running an extra fridge consumes energy—but not nearly as much as is needed to process, package, and ship the crops you would buy otherwise.

Crop	Peak Season	Handling and Storage Tips
Apples	Late summer to fall	Late maturing tart apples store best. Ideal temperature range is 30 to 40 degrees with high humidity. Separate apples from root vegetables because they give off ethylene gas that causes veggies to spoil. *(May also be dried or canned.)*
Beets	Summer to to fall	With tops removed, unwashed beets will keep 3 months or more at 32 to 40 degrees with high humidity. *(May also be canned.)*
Brussels sprouts	Fall	Pull up plants, shake soil from roots, and hang upside down in a cool basement. They will keep 3 to 6 weeks at 40 degrees with high humidity. *(May also be frozen.)*

Crop	Peak Season	Handling and Storage Tips
Cabbage	Late summer to fall	Plants dug, trimmed, and replanted in large pots will keep up to 7 months at 32 to 40 degrees with high humidity. Trimmed heads will keep 3 months. *(May also be canned.)*
Carrots, parsnips	Late summer to fall	Topped roots with leaves snipped off just above the growing crown will keep 3 months or more at 32 to 40 degrees with high humidity. Roots replanted in spring will produce seeds. *(May also be frozen.)*
Onions	Late summer to fall	Cured pungent onions will keep 6 months or more at 32 to 40 degrees with moderate humidity. Sweet onions store 1 to 2 months.
Pears	Fall	Wipe clean, pack in loose paper, and store at 29 to 34 degrees with high humidity. Most varieties store less than 3 months. *(May also be frozen, canned or dried.)*
Potatoes	Summer to fall	Store best at 40 to 45 degrees with high humidity. Varieties will begin sprouting in 3 to 8 months.
Rutabagas	Fall	Will keep 2 to 4 months at 32 to 40 degrees with high humidity.
Sunchokes	Fall, winter, spring	Will store 2 to 5 months at 32 to 40 degrees with high humidity. Can be left in the ground in Zones 6 to 8.
Turnips	Fall	Stretch the fall season with protective covers. Topped roots store 4 months or more at 32 to 40 degrees with high humidity.

FREEZER PLEASERS

Freezing is often the best way to preserve the flavors and textures of delicate vegetables, and small batches can be blanched to stabilize nutrients and texture, cooled to preserve color, then packaged—in 30 minutes or less. Running a freezer consumes energy, but reduced packaging is where the home food preserver comes out on top. For instance, pint-size poly freezer bags or pouches require a quarter less energy to produce than the freezer-proof boxes used for many commercial frozen veggies.

To reduce energy consumption, keep your freezer in a cool basement or garage, and fill vacant spaces with plastic bottles or freezer bags filled with water. Should the power go off, the increased thermal mass from the extra ice will slow the thawing process. Store small items inside larger snap-top plastic boxes so they won't get lost in your freezer.

Crop	Peak Season	Handling and Storage Tips
Asparagus	Spring to early summer	Blanch in boiling water 1 minute, cool on ice and freeze.
Berries	Spring to fall	Rinse well, spin or pat dry, and freeze without blanching. *(May also be dried.)*
Broccoli, cauliflower	Late spring, fall	Blanch in boiling water 1 minute, cool on ice, and freeze.
Cantaloupe	Mid to late summer	Cut into bite-size pieces or make balls. Freeze and use within 2 months.

Crop	Peak Season	Handling and Storage Tips
Chard	Summer to fall	Blanch to wilting point in the microwave, or in boiling water. Cool on ice, drain and freeze in small batches to add to other dishes.
Edamame	Mid to late summer	Simmer pods in salted water 5 minutes, and drain. When cool, remove beans and freeze. Can also be frozen whole.
Eggplant	Late summer to fall	Grill or broil slices seasoned with herbs and salt. Freeze when cool.
Peas	Early summer	Blanch in boiling water 30 seconds, cool on ice, then freeze.
Peppers	Summer to fall	Grill or broil to remove skins before freezing, or leave skins on and blanch halved peppers in boiling water 1 minute, then freeze. *(May also be dried.)*
Snap beans	Summer	Blanch in boiling water 30 seconds, cool on ice, and freeze. *(May also be dried or canned.)*
Spinach	Spring, fall	Blanch to wilting point in the microwave, or in boiling water. Cool on ice, drain, and freeze. Stretch season by growing through winter with protection.
Summer squash	Summer	Grill or broil slices seasoned with herbs and salt. Freeze when cool. *(May also be dried.)*
Sweet corn	Mid to late summer	Cut kernels from cob to save freezer space. Heat just to boiling, cool, and freeze.

DEHYDRATED HEROES

Some of the food crops listed here need brief precooking or other special preparation, but many can be washed, peeled, pared, and popped into a dehydrator. You can also simply dry them in the sun or in a solar dehydrator. (See "Build a Solar Food Dehydrator" at www.motherearthnews.com.)

To even out the moisture levels between different-size pieces, place dried foods in an airtight container in the refrigerator for a few days after drying them. If the pieces soften, dry them a bit more before packing them away in storage. For maximum energy savings, store dried food in reusable airtight storage containers made of glass or plastic. The drying process often intensifies flavors, and dried foods take up little space. Dried foods keep three to six months in a dark room or pantry at cool temperatures, or up to a year in the freezer.

Crop	Peak Season	Handling and Storage Tips
Apples	Dry apples that ripen early, in August and September	Dip quarter-inch-thick slices or rings in ascorbic acid (vitamin C) solution to prevent browning. Dry until leathery and almost crisp. *(May also be frozen, canned, or kept in cold storage.)*
Berries	Summer	Thoroughly rinse and pat dry. Cut large berries in half, then dry until leathery. *(May also be frozen or canned.)*
Cherries	Summer	Slice in half or remove pits with a cherry pitter. Dry until leathery but still pliable. *(May also be frozen or canned.)*

Crop	Peak Season	Handling and Storage Tips
Dry beans	Mid to late summer	Harvest after pods fade to tan. Remove beans from pods, then dry for 1 hour in a 150-degree oven to kill any potential pests.
Fruit leathers	Summer to fall	Purée clean, washed fruits. Pour into jellyroll pan lined with plastic wrap. Dry until leathery, but still slightly tacky.
Grapes	Late summer to fall	Use seedless varieties. Blanch in boiling water 30 seconds to crack the skins, then cool on ice. Dry until leathery, but still pliable. *(May also be frozen or canned.)*
Herbs	Summer	Hang bunches in a warm, well-ventilated room. Store dried leaves whole, and crush just before using. *(May also be frozen.)*
Mushrooms	Spring and fall	Wipe clean with a damp cloth or paper towel, then dry at room temperature until crisp.
Parching corn	Mid to late summer	Harvest mature ears when the husks dry to tan, then finish drying indoors until you can twist the kernels from ears. Break the ears in half before drying to promote air circulation around middle kernels.
Peppers	Late summer to fall	Clean thoroughly, cut into quarter-inch-thick strips or rings, and dry until brittle. *(May also be frozen.)*

Crop	Peak Season	Handling and Storage Tips
Peaches, Plums	Summer	Dip quarters or slices in ascorbic acid (vitamin C) solution to prevent browning. Dry until leathery but still pliable. *(May also be frozen.)*
Snap beans	Summer	Blanch 1 minute, cool, and pat dry. Dry until almost brittle. *(May also be frozen or canned.)*
Summer squash	Summer	Clean thoroughly, cut into quarter-inch-thick slices, and dry until leathery and brittle. *(May also be frozen.)*
Tomato	Summer	Dip in boiling water to remove skins. Cut large tomatoes into rings, or cut smaller ones in halves or quarters. Dry until nearly crisp. *(May also be canned.)*
Vegetable paste	Summer to fall	Purée clean, washed vegetables. Cook over low heat 1 hour to evaporate water. Pour into jellyroll pan lined with plastic wrap. Dry to peanut butter consistency, store in the refrigerator. Use in place of vegetable bouillon.
Whole grains	Summer to fall	After threshing and screening, dry grains in 150-degree oven for 30 minutes to reduce moisture content. Store in airtight, animal-proof containers. *(May also be kept in cold storage.)*

From *Mother Earth News* magazine

Chapter 5
TAKE IT SLOW:
THE ART AND IMPORTANCE OF
LEISURELY MEALS

*U*p until now I've been showing you how to acquire and store sustainable and local food in the easiest, most efficient way. I hope that the time you've saved will not mean more time spent checking your email (ahem) but more time spent at the table with people you love. But as I know too well, it's not always easy to shift into a lower gear. I've eaten my fair share of meals standing up at the counter, while on the phone. Sigh.

If you'd like help slowing down and some company in doing so, look no further than the Slow Food movement, which, as its name might suggest, is antithetical to fast food. Slow Food started in 1986 in Italy when farmer Carlo Petrini rebelled—not merely against the opening of a McDonald's beside the Spanish Steps in Rome but against the very industrial food system that was destroying his country's food traditions and its thousands of food varieties and flavors. Today, the eco-gastronomic movement Slow Food is active in more than a hundred countries and has a worldwide membership of more than 85,000. There are 170 U.S. chapters, or "convivia," to promote local farmers, artisans, flavors, and traditions. "We're a community-building organization," my convivium leader, farmer Dominic Palumbo, explained. "This is about meeting people who share your values and your appreciation for food."

Because of its commitment to community, regionality, and tradition, Slow Food goes hand in hand with local food. The Slows consider consumers to be "co-producers" of their food, along with farmers and cooks. Local chapters encourage members to shop at farmers markets and CSAs, create kitchen gardens, and learn the histories of their local foods. Convivia also organize tastings and seminars and create school seed-to-table programs. Not surprising, the Slows are also active in the conservation of "endangered" foods and traditions. The Renewing America's Food Traditions (RAFT) program of the U.S. arm of Slow Food entails collaboration of education, conservation, and food organizations, with the goal of restoring foods and food traditions that might otherwise vanish. RAFT members recommend that individual convivia "adopt" certain foods or propose them for the "Slow Food Ark of Taste, an international catalogue of foods in danger of extinction." The purpose of the Ark is "saving cherished slow foods, one product at a time." Here are some American foods and drinks in the Ark that might bring a tear to your grandmother's eye (God rest her soul) and titillate the curiosity of an appreciative eater.

- **Handcrafted root beer.** We're talking about the fermented kind, made with sassafras root. My own grandmother made it at Christmastime and stored it in her cellar. Real root beer, I will attest, doesn't taste a whit like its ersatz counterpart sold in cans at the grocery store.
- **Anishinaabeg manoomin.** Don't worry—you can just call it "wild rice," even though it's really an aquatic grass that grows in the Great Lakes region. Food trivia bonus: It's the only grain native to North America. Not surprising, the continued existence of wild rice is threatened by pollution, which is sad because the real stuff—not the stuff cultivated in paddies—is earthy tasting and divine.

- **Pawpaw.** Little known except in a few rural areas, the once-loved but almost-forgotten pawpaw is the largest edible fruit native to our country. According to Slow Food, the big green fruit has a "creamy, custard-like flesh with a tropical flavor, which is often described as a combination of mango, pineapple, and banana."

- **Tupelo honey.** I've heard Van Morrison croon about it, but I've never tasted it, which is too bad. It comes from honeybees that collect nectar from the blossoms of the white Ogeechee tupelo tree that grows along certain rivers in the U.S. Southeast. From the Ark: "It has a pear-like and hoppy aroma and a coveted flavor that fans describe as mild, delicate, buttery, floral, like cotton candy and like rosewater."

- **American artisanal sauerkraut.** Made the old way, this kraut has no added vinegar or cultures; it is fermented and unpasteurized. Fans of this method say it not only tastes better but also has beneficial enzymes that aid digestion. (I'll take a big plate of mashed potatoes and sauerkraut over Rolaids any day.)

To learn more about the Slows or join a U.S. chapter, visit their website (www.slowfoodusa.org) or call 1-877-SLOWFOOD.

These are my own tips for living a slocal (slow and local) life:

- **Say grace.** Even in our era of incredible abundance, food isn't something to take for granted. Our family grace, composed by my husband, is nondenominational:

*Let us offer our thanks for this bounteous food, this
irreplaceable day, the joys and tribulations of our
existence, the beauty of the Earth, and the pleasure
of your company. Amen.*

🐚 **Stimulate the conversation.** At our house, dinnertime
is also a time to share the trials and triumphs of our day.
I often ask my daughter to share something she did for
someone else, even if it's just giving a person a smile.
Sometimes we ask everyone at the table to share something good or something frustrating about his or her
day. My daughter's great-aunt always sets place cards
containing handwritten quotes, which guests read out
loud. When you're planning the seating for your next
dinner party, consider boosting the conversation by seating people next to one person they know and one person
they don't. If you're a guest at a dinner party, try this old
conversation-stimulating trick: After each course, switch
conversation partners. Steer clear of thorny subjects like
religion and politics—talk about food!

🐚 **Make at least one meal a day a sit-down meal with
your family.** Shared meals are few and far between in our
heavily scheduled modern life, but making time for them
is demonstrably worthwhile. A 2007 Columbia University
report revealed that the more frequently teens eat dinner
with their family, the less likely they are to drink, smoke,
or use drugs. Remember that a sit-down meal doesn't
need to be fancy—but the TV does need to be turned off.

- **Make meals social events.** Plan dinner parties, potlucks, dessert parties, wine tastings, or cheese tastings. If you're short on time, meet friends at a restaurant. If you're short on cash, meet for coffee and dessert. Instead of a costly dinner out, meet someone for a long lunch.

- **Make cooking a social event.** Meal preparation shouldn't be drudgery. Involve kids or a partner. Put on your favorite music, pour a glass of wine. Do your holiday baking with a friend, or schedule a holiday cookie exchange party. Ask a relative to show you how to make a family recipe. Ask an elderly neighbor how to put up tomatoes. Turn off the Food Network and take a cooking class. Heck, *teach* a cooking class.

- **Share recipes, which is easier than ever with email.** Don't let family recipes go extinct! Consider compiling a list of family recipes as a holiday gift. Ask guests invited to bridal showers or baby showers to bring a recipe for the bride-to-be or the new mom.

- **Share food.** If you made too many brownies (ha-ha, as if this were at all possible), share them with a neighbor. Overzealous about picking apples? Give them to your child's class. Too many zucchini? Donate them to a food pantry.

A LEISURELY DINNER FOR FRIENDS: A RECIPE

1 small group friends, family, and assorted kids (yes, kids)

1½ hours of cooking time. This seems like a lot, but it can be spread out over a day, or even a few days. Main dishes that can be marinated or prepped ahead of time work well. Have your best friend bring a batch of brownies.

3 to 5 CDs, or 1 loaded iPod of great music. Like the term "local," "great" music is subjective. If your spouse enjoys Joni Mitchell (ahem), be nice and include her along with Willie Nelson and Duran Duran.

1 easy appetizer, such as olives, an assortment of local cheeses and baguettes, or prosciutto with local melon

1 tried-and-true main dish, such as the *Silver Palate Cookbook*'s Chicken Marbella or whatever treasured family recipe you find is always a hit, with an easy side dish such as rice. Use at least one local ingredient.

1 to 3 side dishes. Salads work well for fresh, local ingredients.

Several bottles of nice wine, plus a special drink for the kids (have them make their own lemonade, for example)

1 made-well-ahead-of-time dessert (brownies with local whipped cream are always in season)

1 pot of triple-certified coffee (politically correct, yes, but it's also delicious)

1 dog, constantly underfoot

Bring several adults together in a small kitchen. Don't even try to keep people out of the kitchen at a dinner party. (People want to mill about kitchens; it's one of the well-known but little-understood laws of physics.) Pour the first bottle of wine into mismatched glasses and eat the appetizer. Keep the kids occupied by allowing them to cut flowers from the garden and set the table, using their own best judgment for what goes where and what looks good. Don't forget to feed them some cheese and baguettes to keep their energy up. The table will look crazy, and you'll eat dessert with a soupspoon, but who cares? Discard any tendencies toward perfectionism.

Pop dinner into the oven. If you can remember, set a timer. While dinner is heating, conscript restless kids to spin the salad and whisk the vinaigrette. Assure them that the brownies are coming.

Send kids back into the garden with bug nets or flashlights. Pass the baby around. Refill wine glasses. Remove dog from breadbasket.

Squish adults and kids around a too-small table. Say grace. Serve another bottle of wine with dinner. Eat the dinner. Put the sleepy baby to bed.

Meanwhile, serve older kids desserts and send them back outside to play night-tag with flashlights, or into another room with a jigsaw puzzle.

Take a breather before adult dessert time and let everyone stretch their legs. Allow dog to assume his janitorial duties under the dining room table. Allow guests to help in the kitchen.

Serve dessert on the good china in the living room with coffee. For those guests who aren't driving, pour remaining wine. Let kids fall asleep on the floor.

Notice with astonishment how late it is. After goodbyes (and a promise to share recipes), load as many dirty dishes as you can into the dishwasher and kick it shut. Save the rest for morning.

ASK AN EXPERT
MARC DAVID, AUTHOR OF "THE SLOW DOWN DIET"

Based in Boulder, Colorado, nutritional psychologist Marc David is the author of *Nourishing Wisdom: A New Understanding of Eating* and *The Slow Down Diet: Eating for Pleasure, Energy, and Weight Loss.* He earned his M.A. in the psychology of eating at Sonoma State University of California and trained at Harvard Mind/Body Medical Institute.

So, what's the general idea behind "The Slow Down Diet"?

It's that when we're taught about food and health, the conversation generally centers around nutrition and what you should and shouldn't eat. One of the main principles of *The Slow Down Diet* is that *what* we eat is half the story. The other half is *how* we eat. Are we stressed or relaxed when we eat?

You don't really tell people what to eat?

I don't. I have one nutritional rule across the board: It is simply to eat quality foods.

What do you mean by "quality foods"?

Usually nutrition information and nutrition guidelines that come from experts focus on nutrient value . . . you have to analyze a food's nutritional content. To me that's like trying to analyze the value of a great work of art by looking at the pigments in the paint. Quality food to me means anything that's real—food that falls into the category of real or fresh, or lovingly produced, consciously grown, and environmentally sound.

So you're a fan of sustainable and local food?

Oh, hugely! Sustainably and locally grown to me means quality. Quality is less of a scientific term and more of a soulful term. Quality means real value has gone into it. Food has become such a commodity item—"Let's make as much of it as we can and sell it for the best profit." It's about the economics of exchange and the bottom line. To me, food that has *quality* is food that has been made with a sense of respect for people who eat and how nature and health seem to work. That doesn't mean the food doesn't have fat or sugar. The bottom line is that what we put into the food is what we tend to get out of it.

What's the real reason French women are thin?

It's pretty simple. It's a combination of lifestyle practices that are built into their culture. They eat high-quality food. High-quality also means nutrient dense. They get high-quality fats. Americans tend to get a lot of poor-quality, synthetic, harmful fats. The French diet is low in humanmade toxins. On another level, the French are eating in the optimal state for digestion and assimilation and calorie burning, which is relaxation. Most Americans live in a stressed state.

Can stress make a person fat?

There's no doubt about it. Truth be told, we've known this about for about thirty to forty years. In a nutshell, here's the basic science: When we are in a stress response, the sympathetic nervous system is activated. In a full-blown stress response, digestion is completely shut down. If you are partially stressed, it's partially shut down. When the parasympathetic nervous system is activated, that means we have full digestive and calorie-burning power. Stress robs us of our ability to absorb calories and burn them.

What's Vitamin P?

Pleasure. All organisms on the planet, whether a single-celled organism, a frog, a dog, or a human, have something in common: Evolution has programmed us to seek pleasure and avoid pain. There's no arguing that pleasure is built into who and what we are. We know infinitely more from a scientific perspective about pain physiology that we do about pleasure physiology. That's scary. And when we start to dig into the research, we find that pleasure is a required part of the nutritional experience. When we don't get it, we metabolize a meal less efficiently.

What can I do to slow down and add pleasure to my meals?

The first thing is to give oneself time to enjoy a meal, to create a sense of time and spaciousness. We tend in this culture not to give time to a meal. The average time for lunch in the United States is ten to fifteen minutes. The average time in France is close to a few hours. Slow is a choice. Slow is a state of mind. Slow doesn't mean chewing your food one hundred times. Be there. Enjoy it. Slow means sensual. Slow means present. Slow means yummy. If we eat fast, we can't really know what we ate.

What's your idea of a perfect meal?

It has foods that are high quality, organically grown, fresh, tasteful, fanatically produced with quality in mind, lovingly cooked, lovingly served—and whatever it is, it has lots of olive oil and garlic. It is eaten with friends or loved ones who appreciate it as much as I do. When you're finished, you just feel good.

Chapter 6
HUNGRY HEARTS: SHARING LOCAL AND SUSTAINABLE FOOD

a book about fresh, healthy, local food would not be complete if it didn't address the fact that so many people in the United States go without this kind of food—or even without food at all. According to America's Second Harvest, the nation's largest charitable hunger relief organization, 35.5 million Americans lived in "food insecure" households in 2006, and 12.6 million of them were children. A food insecure household is one in which the people do not always know where they will find their next meal. They are, in a word, hungry.

Although government assistance is available to those in need, it does not guarantee access to fresh food. Food stamps are accepted at some farmers markets, but certainly not all of them. Another program, the WIC Farmers' Market Nutrition Program, helps provide fresh, locally grown fruits and vegetables to participating low-income pregnant, breastfeeding, and non-breastfeeding postpartum women, and to at-risk infants and young children. While this is a step in the right direction, many people with limited incomes do not live near farms, farmers markets, or grocery stores or have access to transportation to get to these places. Even if they want sustainable and local food, they cannot necessarily get it. And these foods can also be expensive in comparison to readily available, cheap processed food and fast food.

What can we all do to make sure that everyone not only has food security but also has access to sustainable and local food?

- Make a donation in time, in money, or in kind. In 2007, demand at food pantries across the United States rose sharply, causing many of them to cut back on portions or to close their doors. The cause was a perfect economic storm:

rising cost of living; less surplus food available from retailers, wholesalers, and food manufacturers; and decreased government assistance. So help out. To find a food pantry near you, go to the website for America's Second Harvest, which has a pantry locator searchable by zip code (www .secondharvest.org). Some pantries may accept fresh food. If you do donate nonperishable goods to a pantry, make sure the food is not past its expiration date. Call the pantry; they can tell you what foods are most needed. Lastly, support pantries year-round, not just during the holidays. It's not hard to make a difference. My daughter's first-grade teacher, Susan Frantz, encourages her class (and their parents) to make food pantry donations a habit. The kids collect food donations for local pantries every month. My husband, inspired by first graders, started a food drive at his office.

- If you want to make a monetary donation that goes toward fresh, healthy food, contact a local CSA and ask about donating a share for a needy family.

- Start a community garden. Gardens ease the strain on people's food budgets and are a source of empowerment, relaxation, and community building. Donate surplus from that garden to pantries that accept fresh produce. The American Community Gardening Association is an excellent resource for starting community gardens. The ACGA store also offers a variety of books to help you get started (www.communitygarden.org).

- Read Mark Winne's book *Closing the Food Gap: Resetting the Table in the Land of Plenty*. Winne takes on America's classist food system and offers solutions he helped pio-

neer in Hartford, Connecticut, including partnering with
farmers to make local, organic food available to the poor.

Get inspired. Never underestimate the power of innovation.
The Food Project (www.thefoodproject.org) works with over
a hundred teens and thousands of volunteers to farm 31
acres in suburban Lincoln, Massachusetts, and on several
lots in urban Boston. Each season the project grows nearly
a quarter of a million pounds of food without chemical pesticides, donates half to local shelters, and sells the
remainder through a CSA. In New York City, City Harvest,
a nonprofit organization that "rescues" millions of pounds
of excess food from restaurants and grocery stores, also
practices "gleaning" on farms in the region and pays farmers to harvest surplus crops for the needy. In Tennessee, the
Mobile Farmers Market of Greene County gives people with
limited transportation a chance to purchase fresh, locally
grown produce while giving local farmers another outlet to
sell produce. This market comes in the form of a minibus
staffed by volunteers who visit low-income neighborhoods
and the elderly. The bus is handicapped accessible, and the
organizers accept food stamps.

Advocate for a fair Farm Bill. This bill sets our agricultural
policy, but it isn't just about rural communities. It affects
the environment, trade, and hunger. Advocates for a fairer
bill want to rename it the "Food Bill" and are lobbying to
change it so that it provides fresh food for everyone
instead of subsidizing processed, unhealthy food and special interests. To learn more by watching an apple battle a

Twinkie, go to the Farm Bill Food Battle website (www
.foodbattle.org). Also read Daniel Imhoff's book *Food
Fight: The Citizen's Guide to a Food and Farm Bill.*

- Learn more. The Community Food Security Coalition
  (CFSC) is dedicated to creating sustainable and local food
  systems that ensure that *everyone* has access to healthy
  and culturally appropriate food. CFSC has over 200 member organizations. Its website has a large number of informative publications that can be downloaded or purchased
  (www.foodsecurity.org).

- Eat less meat. Reducing the amount of animal protein in
  your diet helps your heart and might help save the world.
  Meat-eating increases world hunger because a large
  portion of our resources—water, land, and crops—is used
  (and often polluted) for the purpose of feeding livestock.
  An arguably better use would be growing cheaper, less
  resource-intensive grains and other foods for hungry
  people. Food for thought: According to an article in the
  New York Times ("Rethinking the Meat Guzzler" by Mark
  Bittman, January 27, 2008), 800 million people currently
  suffer from hunger or malnutrition worldwide. Meanwhile, most of the corn and soybeans grown in the world
  feeds livestock, not people. It has been estimated that
  reducing meat production by a mere 10 percent in the
  United States alone would free enough grain to feed 60
  million people. You don't have to be a vegetarian or a
  scientist to understand that a meat-based diet is bad for
  our steamy little planet.

🌱 What to do if you're a meat lover like me? Start by working in a few meat-free meals a week and see how you feel—spiritually and physically. *Vegetarian Times* magazine, in print and online, is a great source for recipes (www.vegetariantimes.com). And, of course, when you do purchase meat, purchase it as thoughtfully as possible, and try to buy sustainable and local meat. If I can't buy my meat locally, I look for the USDA Organic label *and* the Certified Humane label. When I eat out and I'm faced with a menu full of cheap meat options, I choose something vegetarian, such as pasta.

VEGETARIAN OPTIONS FOR LACTO-OVO-PESCO-MEATO-TARIANS

So sue me: I don't like frozen veggieburgers. A fresher, "meatier" option is a portobello burger instead of a hamburger. I sauté portobello caps (gills removed) with garlic, olive oil, and a splash of balsamic vinegar. This stand-in for meat can be easily "accessorized" with local bread, lettuce. and tomatoes. When it comes to adding vegetarian meals to my weekly lineup, I don't think too hard about it—I just take the meat out of the recipe and substitute something else. Admittedly, this is hard to do with pot roast, but it's easy to do with many pasta dishes, enchiladas, soups, and sandwiches. At the end of the chapter are recipes for two of my favorite vegetarian switcheroo meals.

ASK AN EXPERT
REVEREND CLARE BUTTERFIELD,
EXECUTIVE DIRECTOR OF FAITH IN PLACE

Clare Butterfield is a Chicago-based Unitarian minister and the executive director of Faith in Place, an organization that gives religious people the tools to become good stewards of the earth. Faith in Place is a partner in the Sacred Food Project, an interfaith effort designed to improve the social and environmental conditions of our nation's food system (www.faithinplace.org).

You talk to people about how conventional food is at odds with moral traditions, and you expose the conditions in which meat and other foods are produced today. How is this received?

It's not initially welcome news. I'm probably messing up a trip to the grocery store that's already a hassle. But I tell people that this is about living in communion with people you don't know.

How so?

I can't ask someone to poison himself so I can have a flawless apple at a cheap price. It's not moral.

How do you eat? Are you a vegetarian?

I eat locally grown, humanely raised, organic meat from a co-op we started. I live with the recognition that an animal gave its life. I also accept that vegetarianism is an appropriate moral choice.

You have used the term "food desert" to describe certain neighborhoods. What does that mean?

People who live in them don't have meaningful access to healthy, fresh, culturally appropriate food.

What can churches do to address hunger issues while working with sustainable and local food?

Some day, some great day, we have to rebuild our food system so that all of us eat primarily from local sources. A congregation is a stepping-stone from here to there. A congregation can start a CSA. Why not have extra shares for those who can't afford to participate?

Does your congregation really serve triple-certified coffee after the service?

Oh, yes. That's a good first order of business for any congregation.

How often does your congregation eat together?

All the time. Food is something that is universally understood—a way for human beings to come together to know each other.

RED SAUCE FOR ENCHILADAS

My vegetarian enchiladas are always made from left-overs: usually beans, rice, and squash (fresh and local), rolled into tortillas and topped with sauce and organic cheese. If I have enough time, I make a homemade chile sauce. Once you've lived in New Mexico, you can't open a can of enchilada sauce without a little sigh of disappointment. So here's a quick recipe for the real deal.

> 2 cups vegetable stock (mea culpa—as a carnivora, I also use chicken stock)
> 3 tablespoons canola oil
> 3 tablespoons flour
> 2 teaspoons (or more, according to taste) good red chile powder, such as Chimayo
>
> *Yield: Approximately 2 cups, enough for 8 to 10 enchiladas*

Warm stock in a saucepan over low heat. In a heavy-bottomed skillet, heat canola oil over medium-high heat. Whisk in enough flour to make a thick paste. Keep stirring. (Look at you! You are making a roux!)

Continue stirring over medium-high heat for about a minute as the paste bubbles and browns slightly. Stir in red chile powder to taste. Start with two teaspoons. Immediately add a splash of warm stock. Stir vigorously to remove the lumps.

Keep adding stock, a little at a time, while vigorously stirring out the lumps. As the roux thins into a sauce, you can add the rest of the liquid. The finished sauce will be smooth and silky. Turn heat down to low and simmer for about 15 minutes, stirring occasionally. Add more liquid and more salt if necessary.

Note: Red chile powder is not powdered cayenne or paprika. And it varies, a lot, from place to place, even in New Mexico (it is a quintessentially local food!). If you want the real deal, find a Mexican market or good gourmet store and tell the staff exactly what you are making—they'll give you the good stuff. (Better yet, get friends in New Mexico to mail you some chile powder from their market.) Then, experiment with how much chile powder to add to your sauce to get the flavor and heat you want.

PESTO SAUCE FOR PASTA

Fresh pesto is ridiculously easy to make, and as an added bonus the combination of pine nuts with pasta and cheese forms a complete protein. Here's our recipe. My daughter likes to lick the spatula as if it were cookie batter.

1 big bunch (about 2 cups lightly packed) fresh basil leaves, washed

$^1/_2$ teaspoon salt

2 to 3 ounces Parmigiano-Reggiano cheese, grated

2 or 3 cloves fresh garlic, peeled

3 to 4 ounces pine nuts

2 to 3 tablespoons extra-virgin olive oil—the best you can afford

Yield: Enough for about 2 pounds of spaghetti (6 to 8 servings)

Put basil, salt, cheese, garlic, and pine nuts into a food processor and blend for about a minute, stopping intermittently to scrape sides. Then, with processor running, drizzle in olive oil to make a thick paste.

Optimally, you should make and serve the pesto immediately—it will not keep even ten minutes without beginning to oxidize. However, you can keep it for a day or two in the refrigerator in a sealed container. Be sure to top the stored pesto with a layer of olive oil. This will keep it from turning an unappetizing shade of brown and becoming bitter. Pesto also freezes well, cheese and all.

Chapter 7
TURN, TURN, TURN: SEASONAL EATING AND DRINKING

his much we know: For most of human history, our very survival depended on seasonal eating, which in turn relied on foraging successes, crop successes, and the mercy of the weather. Even though life in America no longer depends on it, seasonal eating is still worth the effort. Flavor is at its peak when a food is freshly harvested. At least as important, though, is the sheer pleasure of the rituals that correspond with seasonal eating. If your seasonal menu-planning skills are a bit rusty (I can never remember when cantaloupe is in season), look to the following resources.

- **The Internet.** The Sustainable Table can help you find what's in season in most states (www.sustainabletable.org/shop /eatseasonal). Also try your state's Department of Agriculture, which may provide a list of produce that's in season. Find your state ag department through the National Association of State Departments of Agriculture (NASDA), www.nasda. org. For seasonal recipe ideas online, try Harvest Eating, a website that celebrates seasonal, local, and organic foods. Find recipes and watch videos of chef Keith Snow preparing seasonal dishes (www.harvesteating.com).
- **Cookbooks.** There are lots of great cookbooks to motivate you to make the most of each season's peak flavors, so cruise your local bookseller's cookbook section. My favorite, for both its luscious recipes and its good writing, is *Local Flavors: Cooking and Eating from America's Farmers Markets* by Deborah Madison. Here's my tip for finding seasonal cookbooks: Go to Amazon.com's "Listmania" search function to check out the lists that voracious

cooks and foodies have compiled. (Punch in keywords such as "seasonal cooking.") Once I find a book I like, this thrifty gal requests it at her local library. If after careful review, I can't live without it, I order it from a local book-seller or buy it used.

TO EVERYTHING (EVEN MEAT) THERE IS A SEASON

Seasonality! It's not just for produce. There's also a best time to buy meat and eggs, especially if you're buying from small producers.

- **Eggs:** Small-scale egg producers may experience fluctua-tions in the quantity of the eggs they sell. Egg production can decrease for any number of reasons, including the age of the hen, but it generally decreases in the winter, al-though even small producers may use lights to increase egg production during shorter days. A little note on freshness: If you can't get farm-fresh eggs, use them by the date on the package. FYI, eggs will keep for about three to five weeks in your refrigerator. If there's any doubt about freshness, put your eggs in a deep pot of water. If an egg floats, toss it! This isn't old-wives'-tale nonsense; there's an air pocket inside that increases with the age of the egg.
- **Chickens** generally are slaughtered from late spring into early autumn. If you want a fresh chicken, call ahead. (Your farmer may keep frozen chicken on hand year-round.) If you want a local bird for Thanksgiving, place your order well ahead of time. Call your farmer in late summer or early fall and get yourself on the list. To find sustainable poultry near you, try the American Pastured

Poultry Producers Association (APPPA) "producers network" on its website, www.apppa.org.

- **Cattle** typically are slaughtered in late summer or fall. Farmers may have frozen meat available anytime, but if you want dibs on premium cuts, order ahead. Some farms sell variety packs of meat that include ground beef, premium cuts, and rump roasts; others may sell you a whole, half, or quarter side of beef, which is an economical option if you have the freezer space. Another money-saver is sharing a side of beef with a friend or group of friends. To find a local and sustainable beef producer, try Eat Wild (www.eatwild.com) or the American Grassfed Association's website, www.americangrassfed.org.

- **Pigs** often are slaughtered in the fall, but may be slaughtered year-round. Again, you may have the option to buy a large portion of the animal.

- **Lambs** are slaughtered in both spring and fall. If you love lamb, consider buying a whole animal. (Try Eat Wild to find local lamb, too.)

If you encounter an unfamiliar cut of meat, look at it as a culinary adventure! Then consult your *Joy of Cooking* or your local butcher for advice.

LOCAL AND SUSTAINABLE HOLIDAY MEAL PLANNER
January
Happy New Year! Should auld acquaintance be forgot? Well, yes, if it means you start the New Year out with nothing but packaged, out-of-season foods. This year, serve local bubbly, which, unless you live in the Champagne region of France, cannot be called Champagne and will be called sparkling wine (or, in some circles, "nose fizz"). Consider noshing on a local cheese plate after the ball drops. Do you live somewhere where citrus is in season? Make a mimosa for me. For New Year's Day, make a batch of Hoppin' John (a traditional New Year's Day dish in the American South), and throw in a resolution to join a CSA this summer. Serve the Super Bowl crowd a local beer and nachos topped with salsa you made with tomatoes from your garden last summer.

February
There is no bigger expression of love on Valentine's Day than an organic chocolate torte made with local cream and topped with a purée of summer-foraged berries from your freezer. (Okay, there are bigger expressions of love, but work with me here.) Also this month, don't forget about Mardi Gras: *Laissez les bon temps rouler* with gumbo made with sustainable seafood (my husband makes a version that includes local sausage)

or a vegetarian jambalaya spiced up with dried herbs from your garden. Dig some pecans out of the freezer (the best place for long-term nut storage) and make pralines to munch with Fair Trade coffee. Or earn your beads the tame way by making fresh, hot beignets (Say it with me the American way: BEN-YAYS). The recipe I use is at the end of this chapter. If you can't go local, use the highest-quality ingredients possible. I've included my local ingredients to show how even a doughnut can be local.

March

While the weather is still lion-ish, get some fresh maple syrup (I like un-fancy B-grade because it's darker and more maple-y) for pancakes made with real eggs and organic milk (not to mention that great King Arthur flour, if you live in the Northeast). For St. Patrick's Day, skip the green beer and serve a local brew with a classic corned beef dinner (use one of those rump roasts you got from your local farmer and have been squirreling away in your freezer). *Hint:* If you don't wash cabbages when you store them, they may keep for several months. *Q:* Have you started your seedlings?

April

Why buy local eggs for your Easter egg hunt? Because you can make divine egg salad later. Please note: You don't need pure white eggs for dyeing. My daughter and I dip light brown and pale green farm-fresh eggs in Paas Easter-egg dyes and they look beautiful! For Easter dinner, check Eat Wild (www.eatwild. com) to find pastured spring lamb in your area and serve it with mint sauce. Spearmint, by the way, is a hardy perennial and a great addition to iced tea when the weather gets warmer—which, I promise, will happen.

May

Why not throw a party for the "most exciting two minutes in sports," the Kentucky Derby, which happens on the first Saturday in May? Do as I do and root for the underdog while sipping on mint juleps made with fresh mint if you can get it. May is also home to Mother's Day, the brunchiest day of the year. Let Mom sleep in while you whip up omelets with the quintessential spring vegetable: asparagus. Add a splash of local cream to her coffee. Consider giving her an edible plant, such as a potted herb, for Mother's Day. For the Memorial Day cookout: sausage made from local pork, early greens from the garden, and, if you're in the right growing zone, local new potato salad.

June

Celebrate the arrival of summer and the end of the school year with strawberry shortcake made from U-pick berries and local cream. Gather inspiration and ingredients for local meals at the farmers markets, which are starting to thrive this time of year. For Father's Day, make waffles for the big guy, topping them with a strawberry/rhubarb compote. For the dad who loves the manly art of grilling, check with farmers who may have fresh chicken. If you're out of luck, ask your fishmonger about sustainable wild salmon, which is now in season.

July

If you're making grass-fed burgers for your Independence Day cookout, good for you, but turn that grill down. Grass-fed meat, which is higher in healthy omega-3 fats and lower in saturated fat than corn-fed stuff, needs a lighter touch and shouldn't be overcooked. My favorite Fourth of July tradition: Getting out the hand-crank ice cream maker and putting the half-pints to work on fresh pints. My husband grew up with a White Mountain ice cream freezer, and we got a new one after we had kids. Don't buy the electric version! Ice cream tastes better when the little folks have really had to work for it (adults, too). And go ahead, let them lick the dasher! Now is the season for gardener burnout, but don't give in: Keep weeding.

August

Don't plan that clambake at the beach house without boning up on sustainable seafood. Check out the Monterey Bay Aquarium's regional seafood guides (www.mbayaq.org/cr /seafoodwatch.asp), which give the latest information on sustainable seafood choices available in different regions of the United States. *Tip:* Escape the summer heat by thinking ahead to frostier times; plan a late-season garden by planting hardy greens (lettuces, spinach, tatsoi) under a simple cold frame you'll close up later.

September

Here's a Labor Day picnic—a couple of baguettes from your local bakery, an array of local cheeses, fresh wild berries that you foraged for, a salad made from greens from the farmers market (or your own garden!), pasta salad with the last of the season's tomatoes, apple crumble (no crust necessary) from in-state apples. If you live in a region with local winemaking—and more Americans do than ever before—consider hosting friends for a tasting. Back-to-school lunch thoughts: Ditch the vinyl lunchbox. Pack local fruit. Warm healthy dinner leftovers and shove them into a stainless steel thermos. Make cupcakes for the first day of school.

October

Boo! At your Halloween party serve local apple cider (spiked with rum for the grown-ups) and caramel apples (my favorite local apple is a Mutsu, a huge green orb that we find at a nearby hillside orchard). Look for harvest fairs and Octoberfests this time of year. For pumpkins and apples, try to find a U-pick farm. For the kids, look for hayrides and corn mazes. *Bottom line:* It's a great time of year for farm-going!

November

Hey, why not start out the baking season with some *pan de muerto,* a sweet bread that is baked and enjoyed on *El Día de los Muertos* (Day of the Dead), a holiday marked in Mexico on November 1. Far from creepy, this holiday is very much a celebration. Families remember their loved ones with beautiful altars and special foods such as elaborate sugar skulls. Moving on: Thanksgiving = locavore heaven! Go for a local heritage-breed bird if you can. If you don't have any local turkey farmers in your part of the world, try LocalHarvest (localharvest .org or Heritage Foods USA (www.heritagefoodsusa.com), and order up a fat, tasty Bourbon Red for your table. Speaking of bourbon, parsnips are sweet this time of year: I purée mine and add butter and some of that fine Kentucky firewater. If your Turkey Day gathering involves adventurous friends, consider challenging them to bring a dessert or side dish with at least one local ingredient in it. Entrants could be pumpkin pie made with local pumpkin (not as hard as it sounds), a dressing made with local nuts, mashers with chives from somebody's garden, or squash soup from farmers market squash.

December

Happy Holidays! Relax (um, yes, relax) by baking with friends, or plan an old-fashioned cookie exchange party. Consider making edible gifts—my husband makes coveted double-chocolate biscotti for friends and family. One year I made very funny but considerably less-refined gingerbread outhouses, which were a big hit. For your Christmas ham, consider heritage pork served with a seasonal ale. If you're making latkes for Hanukkah, use local or organic potatoes, onions, and eggs. Consider gifts of local food or farm crafts this season: honey, soap, beeswax candles, jams, jellies, dried herbs, olive oils, or even a subscription or donation to a nearby CSA. And just think: no shipping! If you can, go to a Christmas tree farm and cut your own. *Thrifty tip:* Christmas trees can be a bit pricey. We make our front-door wreath out of the boughs we've trimmed from the bottom of the tree. Last, serve a hot cocoa that will make you a legend among children. And your friends. And your spouse. See the recipe at the end of this chapter.

FINDING LOCAL WINES

Johnny Depp allegedly had a tattoo on his arm that said "Winona Forever." After his breakup with fellow actor Winona Ryder, he had it changed to "Wino Forever." This is not only funny but also completely understandable, since Depp lives in France, where some of the best wines in the world are produced.

Okay, that story was just fun to tell. My point: Although France produces great wines, it's worth your time to check out the wines in your state (and, as of early 2008, every state in the continental United States is home to wineries), even if that state isn't California or if the local wine doesn't taste like a Château

Lafite Rothschild. A trip to a local winery is a great way to spend an afternoon and get out of a big-name wine rut. And of course, meeting the vintner allows you to ask how the wine was made. Because conventionally grown grapes get a triple whammy when it comes to sprays—insecticides, fungicides, herbicides— more and more consumers want organic wine that is produced from organically grown grapes. They also want wines with no added sulfites. The preservative sulfur dioxide causes an allergic reaction in some people. (Even organic wines are not sulfite free, though, because some sulfites occur naturally.)

Here's how to find local wine:

- If you want to explore the wine in your own state, WineAmerica's Trailblazer Program gives you the tools to find more than 800 member wineries in 48 states (www. wineamerica.org). To find wine tastings and festivals in your area, try www.localwineevents.com.
- Read *Wine Across America: A Photographic Road Trip* by Daphne Larkin and Charles O'Rear. Larkin and O'Rear logged 80,000 miles and visited many of America's 5,000 wineries. They visited "pioneers" in every state: people who grow grapes in varied climate and soil conditions and make wine in everything from fancy estates (Napa) to converted potato barns and fire stations. Their road trip is captured in 300 wonderful color photographs that will inspire you to take a chance on, and make a trip for, local wine.
- Do you dream of becoming a winemaker but you can't afford wine school or a vineyard of your own? The Sannino Bella Vita Vineyard on Long Island, New York, has a Home

Winemakers Center that will give you the opportunity to get hands-on winemaking experience "from vine to wine." For a fee of $3,500, the winemakers provide the equipment, knowledge, and grapes to help you produce your own barrel (275 bottles) of wine that you will also bottle and label (www.sanninovineyard.com). If armchair winemaking is more your speed, try my favorite wine book in the whole entire wild world—*The Grail: A Year of Ambling & Shambling Through an Oregon Vineyard in Pursuit of the Best Pinot Noir Wine in the Whole Wild World* by Brian Doyle. It's a smart, funny, in-depth look at winemaking that will give you a healthy respect for the hard work that goes into a bottle of pinot noir.

- Look locally: While thumbing through my tiny weekly newspaper I came across an ad for something called "Stingy Jack's pumpkin wine." Intrigued, the hubby and I loaded the kids in the car and drove out to the countryside, where we idled away a few hours at the tiny vineyard and tasting room of Les Trois Emme, a family-run winery in New Marlborough, Massachusetts. The pumpkin wine, as we discovered through a tasting, is white wine subtly infused with pumpkin and spices, packaged in a shockingly bright orange bottle. Was it a high-end wine? Was it organic or made from entirely local grapes? No on all counts. But talk about a "wow" hostess gift!

- Have your first crush. Want to experience the full seasonality of wine? Ask a local winery if you can volunteer during the busy autumn harvest season. You may be asked to pick grapes, remove MOG (material other than grapes) from grape clusters, clean equipment, or do other essential tasks.

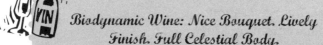

Biodynamic Wine: Nice Bouquet. Lively Finish. Full Celestial Body.

According to the Center for Urban Education about Sustainable Agriculture (www.cuesa.org/sustainable_ag/glossary.php), biodynamic farming is based on the work of Austrian philosopher Rudolf Steiner: "In addition to organic practices such as crop rotation and composting, biodynamic farmers rely on special plant, animal and mineral preparations and the rhythmic influences of the sun, moon, planets and stars." Why is this a good thing for your wine? Think of biodynamic as über-organic. Because biodynamic growers are so fully committed to working with nature (the soil and farm are considered living organisms), a certified biodynamic vineyard in all likelihood will exceed organic standards. For more information, try the Biodynamic Farming and Gardening Association website (www.biodynamics.com).

HANDCRAFTED BEER, AND OTHER PROOF
THAT GOD LOVES US

If beer is your grown-up beverage of choice, the best place to find a local mug of foamy goodness is a microbrewery or a brewpub, which will serve handcrafted beer with its food. The Association of Brewers reports that in 2006 there were 1,389 regional craft breweries, microbreweries, and brewpubs in the United States. Because the beer is made on the premises, you may be able to take a peek at the brewing process. While you're there, check out which seasonal brews are on tap. In the fall, look for Octoberfest beers (pale lagers) or special autumn beers that may be infused with pumpkin pie spices. (If you need a break from beer, try hard cider—the alcoholic version of apple cider.) For winter brews, consider heavy, comforting beers that go with stews, like stouts and brown ales, or Belgian-style lambic beers. Also keep an eye out for specialty Christmas ales, but be aware that these can pack a punch in terms of alcohol content. In spring and summer, go for lighter, hoppier beers such as India Pale Ales (IPAs) or wheat beers, which may arrive with a slice of lemon. Of course, be on the lookout for organic beers made from organic barley, hops, and yeast. Extra bonus points if the hops are grown in the United States! Here's a good source if you need more specifics: www.beerinfo.com/index .php/pages/beerstyles.html.

For tips on pairing brews with food and to find a brewery near you, try the Brewers Association site Beertown.org (www.beertown.org), which has a U.S. Brewery Locator. Also try the Beer Info website, www.beerinfo.com/index .php/index.html.

- If there's no brewpub or microbrewery in your town, try your grocery, natural foods store, co-op, or liquor store for in-state beers (and wines), some of which may be organic. Can't find an organic, local beer at all, and you're the do-it-yourself type? Don't worry, be hoppy; become a home brewer. Order supplies from Seven Bridges Cooperative (www.breworganic.com).

- Some breweries offer refillable 64-ounce glass containers called "growlers." By refilling my growler at my local brewpub, The Barrington Brewery, I not only get a discount on beer, but I also eliminate the packaging associated with a six-pack.

- If you're interested in how today's American beer renaissance "champions ecologically sustainable production, and is helping to create thriving community places," as well as how women were historically involved with brewing beer, read *Fermenting Revolution: How to Drink Beer and Save the World* by Christopher Mark O'Brien.

TIP: What can you make from a local potato besides a nice batch of garlic mashers? Vodka. And I'm not talking hooch here, I'm talking about handcrafted stuff that would make Eastern Europeans weep with appreciation. While there aren't many "craft distilleries" yet (in 2008, fewer than 150 by some estimates), the number is growing, and mark my words: The next big thing in the eat-local movement will be cocktails. Expect martinis made with local vodka or gin, margaritas made from local tequila, or a nice glass of brandy or local fruit liqueur. For a directory of craft distillers, try the American Distiller website (www.distilling.com).

BEIGNETS

$^1/_2$ cup local butter (mine comes from nearby High Lawn Farm)

1 teaspoon sugar (use maple sugar for extra points in New England)

$^1/_4$ teaspoon salt

1 cup water (filtered and, of course, local)

1 cup plus 2 tablespoons sifted flour (I use King Arthur flour, which is from Vermont)

1 teaspoon vanilla (this is locally sourced, if not locally grown; it's from Charles H. Baldwin & Sons, in West Stockbridge, Massachusetts)

4 eggs (from North Plain Farm, three miles away)

Canola oil (not local, but organic)

Confectioners' sugar (not local, but organic)

Yield: Serves 4 to 6, fewer if one person is a very, very hungry mom

In a medium saucepan, heat butter, sugar, salt, and water until mixture boils. Remove from heat and add flour; stir vigorously until combined and the doughy batter pulls away from the sides of the pan. Add vanilla, then eggs, one at a time, stirring vigorously until you have a smooth and glossy batter.

In a separate, high-sided pan (I use a cast-iron Dutch oven), heat about $1^1/_2$ inches of canola oil to 375°F on a candy thermometer. Drop heaping teaspoons of batter into the oil and fry beignets, a few at a time, until they form golden puffballs (they will float, and you may have to turn them over). Drain on plates covered with paper towels.

Give each beignet a generous dusting of confectioners' sugar and eat them while they are warm. I serve mine with locally roasted Barrington Coffee organic French Roast.

RUBINESQUE HOT CHOCOLATE

This recipe came from the cheerful baristas at Rubi's, a café in my town that is adjacent to Rubiner's Cheesemongers & Grocers, a gorgeous cheese shop and gourmet grocery. Rubi's supports local food and farmers, and I'm a regular there. (Okay, I'm a big-time loiterer!) The following recipe is a slight variation on theirs, as close as I could get without a fancy-schmancy steamer. The Valrhona cocoa is French, made from the best chocolate beans, and worth every penny! What can I say? Some women spend money on shoes. I spend it on cocoa. So where the heck is Little Miss Local going with this train of thought? If I'm going to buy a long-distance food (alas, cocoa will never be local for most of us), I try to buy Fair Trade, organic, or super-duper high quality—in other words, a special treat. I also "localize" this cocoa by using High Lawn Dairy products, which come from two towns away.

2 cups half-and-half (I use High Lawn Farm)
$1/3$ cup turbinado sugar
$1/3$ cup Valrhona cocoa powder
A pinch of salt
Filtered local tap water
1 teaspoon Bourbon vanilla (Charles H. Baldwin & Sons)
1 dab butter (High Lawn Farm)
Yield: 2 cups of very rich hot cocoa

In a saucepan, heat half-and-half on the stove over low heat. Whisk it as it heats or it will form a skin, which is decidedly unpopular with the little ones.

Meanwhile, in a glass container (I use a glass measuring cup), mix the turbinado sugar and cocoa. (Turbinado sugar is less sweet than white sugar, and part of the beauty of this hot cocoa is that it is not cloying. If you are using white sugar, cut back a little on the amount.) Add a pinch of salt. Add water, a little at a time, until the mixture is the consistency of syrup. Add vanilla and stir again.

When the half-and-half comes to a simmer, whisk in a dab of (local) butter. Then whisk in cocoa syrup to taste. Go easy—it can be intense! The cocoa should be light brown, but you may be brave enough to go darker. Any leftover syrup will keep in the refrigerator for a few days.

GLOSSARY

A LOCAVORE'S LEXICON

Aeroponic growing system: Space-age technology that is so much better than Tang! A dirt-free growing method in which plant roots are suspended in air within a 100 percent humidity, highly oxygenated growing chamber. Everybody now: Ooooooooooh!

Agritourism: The travel industry defines this as "recreational travel undertaken to agricultural areas or to participate in agricultural activities." Need an example? Touring the vineyards of Napa Valley. Swoon!

Artisanal (aka **handcrafted):** When it comes to food, this term means "made by hand or in a traditional way," such as in small batches. Think un-branded, very high quality, and full of authentic flavor. Think handcrafted beer or chocolates or bread or sausage. I don't know about you, but I'm getting hungry.

Big Organic (aka **industrial organic):** Sobriquet for big-name organic producers such as Horizon Organic and Earth-bound Farm. Why is this term used pejoratively? The fear is that Big Organic will put small organic producers out of business and/or dilute organic standards. It's hard to allay such fears when many Big Organic labels are owned by major corporations that, shall we say, do not have an organic tradition (for example, General Mills owns Muir Glen and Cascadian Farm).

Biodynamic: Organic, and then some. In addition to organic practices, biodynamic farmers use special practices (such as using solar and lunar cycles to plant) and mineral and herbal preparations for the soil (such as burying manure-filled cow horns in their fields). Biodynamic farmers tend to view their land as a self-sustainable organism. Advocates for biodynamic farming and gardening say that the fruit and vegetables it produces are superior to even organic ones.

Bulls: Male cattle, as evidenced by testicles. Avoid petting this animal. FYI: Not all bulls have horns and not all horned cattle are bulls. One of my farmers, Sean Stanton, said the most frequent question he is asked about his horned cattle is "Are all those bulls?"

CAFO: Confined Animal Feeding Operation (aka Concentrated Animal Feeding Operation), which is, according to Sustain-able Table (sustainabletable.org), "an agricultural business where animals are raised in confined situations and fed an unnatural diet, instead of allowing them to roam and graze." These can be huge, containing thousands of

chickens, cattle, or pigs. You may very well hear CAFO as
an adjective: "Oh, ick! A menu full of CAFO meat. I'll be
having the veggieburger!"

Carbon footprint: The measurement of how much carbon
dioxide (CO_2)—a greenhouse gas—your lifestyle produces.
A bigger footprint is harder on the planet. Example: "My
carbon footprint was huge until I sold my SUV!" To check
out your foot size, go to www.carbonfootprint.com.

Certified humane: Technically, it's "Certified Humane Raised
& Handled." When you see this consumer label it means
that your egg, dairy, meat, or poultry product was produced
with the welfare of the animal in mind. Among the
standards for certified humane are that the animal must
have "sufficient space, shelter and gentle handling to limit
stress" and "ample fresh water and a healthy diet without
added antibiotics or hormones." When I can't go to a farm
and see the animals firsthand, I look for this label along
with the Certified Organic label. (For more info, go to the
Certified Humane website, www.certifiedhumane.com.)

Cheap food: In sustainable circles, this is a pejorative term. It's
lousy, mass-produced food that's bad for your body and bad
for the environment. It includes junk food, but it's more than
that: It's packaged, chemical-laden, low-quality food.

Companion plants: You know how sometimes animals such
as dogs or goats are housed with high-strung racehorses
to keep them company? This technique is in the same
vein, but different. Many gardeners swear by companion
planting. According to the National Sustainable Agriculture Information Service (www.attra.org), companion

planting is based on the idea that certain plants can benefit others when planted close by. For example, garlic and other members of the onion family are often used as companion plants for roses because they are thought to deter certain garden pests.

Co-op: In the context of this book, a food cooperative, a member-owned store, or a club in which members buy food in bulk at wholesale prices from cooperative warehouses or retail distributors. In the context of Manhattan real estate, co-ops are run by power-wielding boards that can reject your application to buy an apartment because they don't like your haircut.

Cooperative extension office: A service affiliated with land grant universities, staffed with professionals who can answer questions on farming, gardening, food preservation, and so forth. Also known as an "ag" extension office.

Cows: Female cattle. A young female cow is a heifer. In some breeds of cattle, cows as well as bulls have horns.

CSA: Community Supported Agriculture. According to LocalHarvest, this is a label describing a type of farm "wherein a farmer offers a given number of shares to a community, typically in the spring when the farm's cash flow needs are the highest. Members purchase a share up front, and in exchange receive a box of vegetables each week throughout the growing season." Even though Community Supported Ag is a descriptor, it's often used as a noun. "I just joined the coolest CSA; it sells eggs!"

Ecogastronomy: Thoughtful eating that takes into account
the environmental impact of producing food—along with,
of course, taste.

Factory farming (aka **large-scale farming** or **industrialized agriculture**): In terms of meat, think high output and low cost,
achieved by crowded living conditions that lead to suffering
animals, which in turn require antibiotics to halt the spread
of horrid diseases caused by said inhumanely crowded living
conditions (which is where we started). Hence the common
refrain among many vegetarians: "I stopped eating meat
when I learned what happens to pigs at factory farms."

Fair Trade: Certification applied to a product produced
by farmers, often disadvantaged ones in developing
countries, who receive fair prices and wages for their
products—not just market prices, which can be depressed
by commodity markets. How does this relate to sustainability? Fair Trade also helps farmers with fair labor
practices that are good for humans and the land.

Farm: Land used for agricultural purposes—i.e., food production. I'm not exactly sure how a farm differs from a ranch,
but out West the ranches tend to be bigger and involve
livestock and horses and cowboy hats. And yes, there are
ranchers who use holistic land management practices.

Farm Bill: Daniel Imhoff, author of *Food Fight: The Citizen's
Guide to a Food and Farm Bill,* writes that the Farm Bill is
"essentially a $90 billion per year tax bill for food, feed
and fiber." It is federal legislation, renewed every five
years or so, that doles out subsidies to various agricultural interests and, accordingly, shapes everything from

the landscape to what's in your grocery cart. Advocates like Imhoff want to rename the bill the "Food Bill" and overhaul it to provide money for programs that end hunger and provide fresh food for everyone, instead of subsidizing junk food producers and special interests, which is what it does now.

Farmer: A person who grows your food. Don't think Old MacDonald. Think young MacDonald with a cell phone.

Farmers market: An open-air market where farmers or other food producers sell foods and other items they have produced. Sometimes known as a green market. Many are seasonal; some are permanent. Some producers are organic and sustainable; some are not. You got to Make the Ask, baby.

Farm stand: A roadside stand, permanent or seasonal, where farmers sell their products.

Food miles: The number of miles your food travels to get to your table. Most bandied-about and disturbing food-miles factoid: The average piece of produce in the United States travels roughly 1,300 miles to reach your plate.

Foodshed: I like the definition from the online *Double-Tongued Dictionary:* the area which can, or is sufficient to, provide food for a given location. Example: I live in a region of western Massachusetts referred to as the Berkshires, a fantastic foodshed.

Free range: When it comes to chickens, this term means only that the birds have access to the outside, not that they forage freely in the sunshine. Many, perhaps even most, never set foot outside of the shed.

Gleaning: According to the University of Maine's cooperative extension, this practice of gathering after the harvest goes back at least as far as biblical days. "Field gleaning" refers to the gathering of crops either from fields that farmers have already harvested or from fields where it is not profitable to harvest.

GMO (genetically modified organism): An organism that has had its genetic code altered. The jury is out, scientifically speaking, about whether GMOs are safe in our food supply, and this is why GMO foods are banned in some parts of the world. Until they are proven to be safe, this eater is avoiding GMO "Frankenfoods."

Grass-fed (aka **pastured):** From Colorado Local Sustainability (www.localsustainability.net): Grass-fed, grass-finished, grass-based, or grazing-based is a "production system for grazing (grass-eating) animals such as cows, bison, goats, or sheep, in which the animals spend nearly all their time outside eating grass or other plants in a pasture. They are fed little or no grain. If animals are 100 percent grass-fed, no grain is fed to the animals at any time."

Hardiness zone: The area in which you live as defined by minimum temperatures or frost dates to determine which plants will "winter over" (read: survive) in your area. This system of categorization was developed by the USDA.

Heirloom plant: Like an heirloom rug, only edible! Unlike hybrid plants, which are typically created by large seed companies, heirloom plants come from seeds that are passed down from generation to generation. Many were developed or discovered for commercial use more than a century ago, were almost lost, and are now being revived by gardeners and farmers.

IPM (Integrated Pest Management): A method of controlling pests such as insects in ways that are least harmful to people and the environment. An apple farmer who practices IPM may, among other techniques, plant disease-resistant varieties to help limit the need to spray. My take: It's a step in the right direction, but it's not a guarantee that the practices are sustainable and/or organic. So ask questions.

Kitchen garden: An edible home garden, grown for food, preferably just outside your kitchen door. Talk about reducing your food miles!

Locavore (also localvore): The *New Oxford American Dictionary* declared "locavore" the word of the year in 2007! My def: One who eats, often passionately, close to home.

Mad cow disease: Slang for bovine spongiform encephalopathy (BSE), which is a bit hard to say. In sum, "mad cow" is a brain-wasting disease. According to Sustainable Table (sustainabletable.org), "One way this disease is spread is by feeding the meat from infected cattle to other cattle (meat from infected sheep may also cause the disease). This was a common practice on factory farms until the 1980s and 1990s, when it was outlawed in most countries because it was found to cause BSE. At that time, thousands of cattle believed to have been exposed to BSE were killed to prevent further spread of the disease. Consuming beef from infected cattle can cause a fatal brain-wasting disease called new variant Creutzfeldt-Jakob disease (vCJD) in humans." Pass the grass-fed chili!

Marco Polo exemption: A term created by author Bill McKibben. If you are taking or making an eat-only-local challenge, you might make a Marco Polo exemption and allow for food-related items the Italian explorer would have taken on his way to the Silk Road, such as yeast or salt.

Master Gardener: In exchange for education, Master Gardeners share their time and expertise. Master Gardeners are affiliated with agricultural extension programs.

Microclimate: A specific small area in which climate conditions differ from those of the larger surrounding area. Examples: a garden at the bottom of a hill might be colder because cold air drains downward; a south-facing wall can store heat. In other words, your backyard marches to the beat of a different drummer.

Mother-in-law (MIL for short**):** Beneficial ones can be attracted with wine, while pests are deterred by an uncomfortable guest bed. I'm just saying.

Native plants: My native plant nursery, Project Native, uses this definition: "Those plants that grew in a specific area prior to European settlement." In other words, native plants have real roots. Chortle-chortle.

Nose-to-tail: Popularized by British chef Fergus Henderson, this kind of eating wastes little when it comes to animals. Yep, that means tongue, kidney, brains, etc. Some people think this is just plain gross and trendy, but I think it's respectful. If you're going to kill the animal, why not make excellent use of all of it? That having been said, I am afraid of pig's knuckles in a jar.

Organic: For all intents and purposes, this means that foods grown or produced without chemicals, chemical fertilizers, pesticides, or drugs. The USDA allows gradations of organic in its labeling scheme, which strikes me as like being somewhat pregnant. Nonetheless, to carry the USDA's organic label, organic foods must meet certain standards—for example, farmers can't use synthetic fertilizers, chemicals, or sewage sludge (phew!), and the food can't be genetically modified or irradiated. Organic meat and poultry must come from animals that eat only organically grown feed, and these animals can't be administered hormones or antibiotics. To learn more about the USDA's National Organic Program and standards, go to its web page at www.ams.usda.gov/nop/indexie.htm.

Plough to plate (also **seed to table**): This kind of eating means that the eater is engaged in the growing/producing process. In sustainable circles you might also hear talk of "transparency" or "traceability." It means that you see how your food is produced. Nothing is a secret. You know where your food comes from. Who grew it. How the cows looked. If the chickens were outside being chickens. You get the point.

Raised garden bed: A garden that is built up in some sort of frame so that the soil level is higher than the ground around it. Just the thought should ease your achy back.

Raw milk: Unpasteurized milk. It's illegal to sell in some states but not others. Critics such as the Centers for Disease Control and the Food and Drug Administration say it's unsafe because of the potential for the milk to carry pathogens such as *E. coli,* salmonella, and listeria (all of which are normally killed by pasteurization). Raw milk advocates say raw milk has more flavor and health benefits, thanks to its beneficial bacteria. The scoop: I asked a farmer, who shall remain nameless, what he thought of raw milk. He was all for it, but with this somber caveat: "You had better know who you are buying it from and they had better know what they are doing."

Real food (aka **fair food):** Think food without lots of "inputs." Or chemicals. Or creepy hard-to-pronounce things in it. Think fresh, sustainable, and local food. Opposite of cheap food.

Slocal: Slow (as in "Slow Food," below) *and* local.

Slow: Not just the antonym to fast. "Slow," as in Slow Food, is beginning to mean a way of life that is authentic, thoughtful, mindful, traditional, and of quality. The term is now being applied to architecture and crafts. And life.

Sustainable: Term applied to food produced in ecologically principled ways that can go on and on and on and on because they cause no harm to the earth or its inhabitants—plant, animal, or human.

Traceability: When it comes to food, this principle means that you can literally find the source. Local food has the added benefit of traceability. Why is this good? If you know where your food comes from, you won't be panicked during the next national tainted beef/spinach/bagged lettuce recall, will you?

Transitional: A label that essentially means the farmer is waiting for organic certification, which can take a while. As in, years.

Twinkie question: The largely rhetorical question pondered by foodies, locavores, and ecogastronomes: Is an organic Twinkie a good thing? The question I personally ponder: Can I make a Twinkie using local ingredients?

U-Pick: A farm where you pick the food yourself, which is cost saving for both you and the farmer. The farmer saves on harvesting costs and usually passes the savings on to you by setting a reduced price per pound on what you pick.

Watch list: A list of shellfish and finfish that tells consumers whether or not each item is sustainably harvested and/or whether it's contaminated by pollution such as mercury. Don't leave home without one; our oceans are truly in peril, and mercury poisoning is not a laughing matter.

Whole food: An unrefined or unprocessed food, such as brown rice. (Also Whole Foods: a giant natural food store chain.)

Wild card: A nonlocal food, such as chocolate, that is allowed in an otherwise strictly eat-local diet.

Wild edible: An edible plant not cultivated or propagated by humans.

RESOURCES

WEBSITES
Finding Local Food
Blue Ocean Institute (www.blueoceaninstitute.org)
Chefs Collaborative (www.chefscollaborative.org)
Chowhound (www.chowhound.com)
Consumer Reports Greener Choices eco-labels center
    (www.greenerchoices.org/eco-labels)
Coop Directory Service (www.coopdirectory.org)
Cooperative State Research, Education and Extension Service
    (www.csrees.usda.gov/Extension)
Eat Local Challenge (www.eatlocalchallenge.com),
    (www.eatlocal.net)
Environmental Working Group (www.foodnews.org)
The Farmers Diner (www.farmersdiner.com)
Foodroutes (www.foodroutes.org)

Heritage Foods USA (www.heritagefoodsusa.com/friends/
    restaurants.html.)
The Hundred Mile Diet (www.100milediet.org)
LocalHarvest (www.localharvest.org)
Marine Stewardship Council (eng.msc.org)
Monterey Bay Aquarium (www.mbayaq.org)
National Association of State Departments of Agriculture
    (NASDA) (www.nasda.org)
National Cooperative Business Association (www.ncba.coop)
National Sustainable Agriculture Information Service
    (www.attra.ncat.org)
The New Farm website's "Farm Locator" (www.newfarm.org/
    farmlocator/index.php)
Pick Your Own (www.pickyourown.org/index.htm).
Reusablebags.com (www.reusablebags.com)
Robyn Van En Center for CSA Resources (www.csacenter.org)
The Sustainable Table's "Eat Well Guide" (www.eatwellguide.org)
USDA locator (www.ams.usda.gov/farmersmarkets/map.html)
USDA's CSA page (www.nal.usda.gov/afsic/pubs/csa/csa.shtml)

Gardening

American Community Gardening Association
    (www.communitygarden.org)
American Horticultural Society's Planet Heat Zone Map,
    (www.ahs.org/publications/heat_zone_map.htm)
Arbor Day Foundation updated map (www.arborday.org/
    media/zones.cfm)
Container Gardening Tips (www.containergardeningtips.com)
Edible Schoolyard (www.edibleschoolyard.org)

Farmtoschool.org (www.farmtoschool.org)
FoodRoutes farm-to-college (www.foodroutes.org
     /farmtocollege.jsp)
Institute for Agriculture and Trade Policy Smart guide to
     Smart Plastics (www.iatp.org/foodandhealth)
Kidsgardening.com (www.kidsgardening.com)
Seed Savers Exchange (www.seedsavers.org)
Seeds of Change (www.seedsofchange.com)
Slow Food USA school garden programs (www.slowfoodusa
     .org/education/index.html)
Urban Gardening (www.urbangardeninghelp.com)
USDA's Plant Hardiness Zone Map (www.usna.usda.gov/
     Hardzone/ushzmap.html.)
Wild Ones (www.for-wild.org)
Your Backyard Farmer (www.yourbackyardfarmer.com)

Foraging
Edible Landscaping (www.ediblelandscaping.com)
Russ Cohen (users.rcn.com/eatwild/sched.htm)
Wildman Steve Brill (www.wildmanstevebrill.com)

Storage
National Center for Home Food Preservation (www.uga.edu/
     nchfp/index.html)
USDA's Cold Storage chart (www.foodsafety.gov/~fsg/
     f01chart.html)

Slowing Down
Slow Food USA (www.slowfoodusa.org)

Sharing Food

America's Second Harvest (www.secondharvest.org)
Community Food Security Coalition (www.foodsecurity.org)
Faith in Place (www.faithinplace.org)
The Farm Bill Food Battle (www.foodbattle.org)
Food Project (www.thefoodproject.org)
WIC (Women, Infants and Children) Farmers' Market Nutrition
    Program (www.fns.usda.gov/wic/fmnp/FMNPfaqs.htm)

Seasonal Eating

American Distiller (www.distilling.com)
American Grassfed Association (www.americangrassfed.org)
American Pastured Poultry Producers Association (www.apppa
    .org)
Beer Info (www.beerinfo.com/index.php/index.html)
Biodynamics (www.biodynamics.com)
Brewer's Association (www.beertown.org)
Breworganic.com (www.breworganic.com)
Center for Urban Education about Sustainable Agriculture
    (www.cuesa.org/sustainable_ag/glossary.php)
Eat Wild (www.eatwild.com)
Harvest Eating (www.harvesteating.com)
Local Wine Events (www.localwineevents.com)
Sannino Bella Vita Vineyard (www.sanninovineyard.com)
Wine America (www.wineamerica.org)

BOOKS
Agriculture
Henderson, Elizabeth, and Robyn Van En. *Sharing the Harvest: A Citizens Guide to Community Supported Agriculture*, Revised and Expanded. White River Junction, Vermont: Chelsea Green Publishing Company, 2007.

Imhoff, Daniel. *Food Fight: The Citizen's Guide to a Food and Farm Bill*. Berkeley: University of California Press, 2007.

Winne, Mark. *Closing the Food Gap: Resetting the Table in the Land of Plenty*. Boston: Beacon Press, 2008.

Beer and Wine
Doyle, Brian. *The Grail: A Year of Ambling & Shambling Through an Oregon Vineyard in Pursuit of the Best Pinot Noir Wine in the Whole Wild World*. Corvallis: Oregon State University Press, 2006.

Larkin, Daphne, and Charles O'Rear. *Wine Across America: A Photographic Road Trip*. St. Helena, California: Wineviews Publishing, 2007.

O'Brien, Christopher Mark. *Fermenting Revolution: How to Drink Beer and Save the World*. Gabriola Island, British Columbia, Canada: New Society Publishers, 2006.

Cooking and Food Storage
Chadwick, Janet. *The Busy Person's Guide to Preserving Food: Easy Step-by-Step Instructions for Freezing, Drying and Canning*. North Adams, Massachusetts: Storey Publishing, 1995.

David, Marc. *The Slow Down Diet: Eating for Pleasure, Energy, and Weight Loss.* Rochester, Vermont: Healing Arts Press, 2005.

Madison, Deborah. *Local Flavors: Cooking and Eating from America's Farmers Markets.* New York: Broadway, 2002.

Rodale Food Center, *Preserving Summer's Bounty: A Quick and Easy Guide to Freezing, Canning, Preserving, and Drying What You Grow.* Emmaus, Pennsylvania: Rodale Press, 1998.

Waters, Alice. *The Art of Simple Food: Notes, Lessons, and Recipes from a Delicious Revolution.* New York: Clarkson Potter, 2007.

Foraging

Cohen, Russ. *Wild Plants I Have Known . . . and Eaten.* Essex, Massachusetts: Essex Greenbelt Association, 2004.

Gibbons, Euell. *Stalking the Wild Asparagus.* Chambersburg, Pennsylvania: Alan C. Hood & Co., 2005.

Gardening

Baron, Robert C., ed. *The Garden and Farm Books of Thomas Jefferson.* Golden, Colorado: Fulcrum Publishing, 1987.

Coleman, Eliot. *The Four-Season Harvest: Organic Vegetables from Your Home Garden All Year Long.* White River Junction, Vermont: Chelsea Green, 1999.

Lovejoy, Sharon. *Sunflower Houses: A Book for Children and Their Grown-Ups.* New York: Workman Publishing Company, 2001.

Local Food

Ecumenical Ministries of Oregon, *Portland's Bounty: A Guide to Eating Locally and Seasonally in the Greater Portland and Vancouver Areas.* Portland, Oregon: Author, 2001.

Kingsolver, Barbara, with Steven L. Hopp and Camille Kingsolver. *Animal, Vegetable, Miracle: A Year of Food Life.* New York: HarperCollins, 2007.

Nabhan, Gary Paul. *Coming Home to Eat: The Pleasures and Politics of Local Foods.* New York: W. W. Norton and Co., 2002.

Pollan, Michael. *The Omnivore's Dilemma: A Natural History of Four Meals.* New York: Penguin Press, 2006.

Smith, Alisa, and J. B. MacKinnon. *Plenty: One Man, One Woman and A Raucous Year of Eating Locally.* New York: Harmony Books, 2007.

Schools

Cooper, Ann, and Lisa Holmes. *Lunch Lessons: Changing the Way We Feed Our Children.* New York: HarperCollins, 2006.

Shopping

Vinton, Sherry Brooks, and Ann Clark Espuelas. *The Real Food Revival: Aisle by Aisle, Morsel by Morsel.* New York: Penguin Group, 2005.

Trees

Logan, William Bryant. *Oak: The Frame of Civilization.* New York: W. W. Norton & Co., 2005.

OTHER MEDIA

Magazines

Edible Communities (www.ediblecommunities.com); region-specific, local-food print magazines published throughout the United States and Canada

Grist (www.grist.org); website; environmental news, tips, and humor

Mother Earth News (www.motherearthnews.com); print magazine and website; offers upbeat advice on sustainable and self-sufficient living

Vegetarian Times (www.vegetariantimes.com); print magazine and website; offers vegetarian recipes and lifestyle articles

Films

Jamie's School Dinners (www.jamieoliver.com/dvd)
Naked Chef Jamie Oliver's website sells a DVD of the *Jamie's School Dinners* TV series about improving England's school lunch program through his "Feed Me Better" campaign.

The Meatrix (www.themeatrix.com)
Watch (online) this series of animated *Matrix* spoofs that can show adults and kids about the surreal reality of factory farming.

The Real Dirt on Farmer John (available through Angelic Organics, www.angelicorganics.com)
The DVD is the true story about midwestern farmer John Peterson, whose life and family farm are turned around by the sustainable food movement.

Two Angry Moms (www.angrymoms.org)

Buy the music video or get a screening license for this documentary about angry American moms changing school lunches. You can also find out where to see a screening near you.

Radio

"Deconstructing Dinner" (kootenaycoopradio.com/
deconstructingdinner)
Subscribe to podcasts of this Canadian radio show to learn more about the perils of industrial food and about sustainable alternatives.

INDEX

ABOUT THE AUTHOR

Lou Bendrick is a former newspaper reporter who went on to write funny columns and essays for the *Aspen Times*, *Northern Sky News*, and the *High Country News* syndicate, Writers on the Range. Today she is a columnist for *Grist* online magazine. Her work falls under the oxymoronic category of "environmental humor" and also appears in publications such as *Plenty*, *Whole Life Times*, and *Orion Magazine*. She lives and eats locally in western Massachusetts with her darling husband, author Hal Clifford, their two precocious children, and their uncommonly handsome dog.

Chefs on the Farm:
Recipes and Inspiration from the Quillisascut
Farm School of the Domestic Arts
Shannon Borg, Lora Lea Misterly,
Kären Jurgensen; Photography by
Harley Soltes; Foreword by Tom Douglas
A visually rich tour of an organic farm
where award-winning chefs learn
sustainable food practices

The Salvage Studio:
Sustainable Home Comforts to Organize,
Entertain, and Inspire
Amy Duncan, Beth Evans-Ramos,
Lisa Hilderbrand;
Photography by Kate Baldwin
Inspiration and do-it-yourself sustainable
projects to create a warm and
comforting home

Live Generously: 50 Small Acts That
Make a Big Difference
The Live Generously Project; Edited by
Julie Van Pelt
This compact and thoughtful guide will
inspire you to live more generously in
the world.

Wake Up and Smell the Planet:
The Non-Pompous, Non-Preachy Grist
Guide to Greening Your Day
Grist Magazine; Edited by Brangien Davis
Sustainability is the new bling and Grist
knows how to wear it.